D1293049

FACTS AT YOUR FINGERTIPS

ASIA

Published by Brown Bear Books Limited

An imprint of
The Brown Reference Group plc
68 Topstone Road
Redding
Connecticut
06896
USA

www.brownreference.com

Library of Congress Cataloging-in-Publication Data available upon request.

ISBN-13 978-1-933834-11-5

Author: Derek Hall
Editorial Director: Lindsey Lowe
Project Director: Graham Bateman
Art Director/Design: Steve McCurdy
Editor: Virginia Carter

Printed in Singapore

Picture credits

Cover Images
Front: Terraced rice fields, Philippines (Shutterstock/Styve Reineck)

Back: Petronas Twin Towers, Kuala Lumpur, Malaysia (Shutterstock/Low Wai Tiam)

Page 1: Palmyra, Syria (Shutterstock/Styve Reineck)

Shutterstock:
5 Taolmor; 6/7 Nadejda Ivanova; 8/9 Clara Natoli; 10 Marc C. Johnson; 11 Styve Reineck; 12/13 Joshua Haviv; 14 Oleg Kantor; 15 Olga Kolos;16 Neumann; 28/29 Wong Tsu Shi; 30/31 Photomediacom; 32 Grigory Iofin; 33 WizData, Inc.; 34/35 Craig; 36/37 Maza; 39 Dana Ward; 41 Danish Khan; 42/43 Dario; 44 Paul Cowan; 46 Niels Van; 47 Efremova Irina Alexeevna; 48/49 Albo; 50 Timur Kulgarin; 51 Lakis Fourouklas; 52 Taolmor; 53 Vova Pomortzeff; 55 Bruce Amos; 56 Low Wai Tiam; 57 Vishal Shah; 58/59 Kenny Goh Wei Kiat; 60/61 Ng Wei Keong.

TopFoto.co.uk:
18/19 ©TopFoto; 21 © Roger-Viollet/TopFoto.

CONTENTS

ASIA

Asia is the second largest continent, stretching from Turkey to Japan, Siberia to the Indian subcontinent and to the Philippines. Siberia, however, as part of the Russian Federation, is incorporated into the volume on **Europe**.

Early Peoples

Most people in the world were hunter-gatherers until as recently as 5000 B.C., by which time a significant shift in the way early peoples lived was occurring in Asia. In the Middle East, China, and the Indus Valley crops were grown and irrigated, and animals were domesticated. Pottery, metalworking, and housebuilding grew more sophisticated. By about 6000 B.C. villages had grown into towns—with roads and shops—and by 4000 B.C. the wheel had been invented and writing developed in Mesopotamia (today's Iraq). Some of Asia's earlier civilizations included the Harappan in the Indus Valley, whose pictographic scripts have yet to be deciphered; the Sumerians in the Middle East, famed for their pottery; and the Shang people of China, known for their silk textiles and advanced writing systems. The Yayoi civilization, c. 300 B.C., developed in Japan following the arrival of merchants and settlers from the Chinese mainland.

The early culture of south Asia survives to this day in the sense that Sanskrit (the oldest language of the Indian subcontinent) and the main European languages belong to the same family—the Indo-European languages.

Colonial History

The empire of Alexander the Great (356–323 B.C.) once extended from Persia (today's Iran) to India. In more modern times, however, because of its proximity and because its civilizations were so advanced, Europeans looked to Asia for trade (in items such as spices, silk, and tea). Unlike the Americas and Africa, the continent was not "empty" and therefore not ripe for plunder and exploitation. Even so, after the collapse of the Ottoman Empire in 1918, the British

and French secretly partitioned the Middle East. These two nations were also the colonial masters of the Indian subcontinent and Indo-China respectively, and in northwestern Asia the Russians dominated a number of countries, which formed the old Soviet Union.

Today's Asia

Mention of Asia today tends to mean one of two things: unrest in the oil-rich Middle East, or the burgeoning economies of China and India. Increased globalization and low wages in Asia have led to many household objects being manufactured not in the United States, Germany, Britain, or Japan, but in China and Southeast Asia. "British" cars are produced in China, and "Japanese" cameras are often assembled in Malaysia or Taiwan. With such rapid industrial growth have come fears about pollution and global warming. Although carbon emissions per capita in Asian countries are at present well below those of western Europe and the United States, the size of the population in both India and China means that the problem is likely to increase.

Natural Asia

Asia is home to the Himalayas, the Urals (the latter forming the natural boundary between northern Asia and northern Europe), the Caspian Sea (the world's largest inland sea), the Gobi and Arabian Deserts, the Tibetan Plateau, and the Yangtze, Mekong, Ganges, and Euphrates Rivers. Vegetation varies from the grasslands (steppes) of the north to the temperate forests and rain forests of the south.

The collision of tectonic plates means that Asia can be subjected to earthquakes (in Turkey, Iran, and Japan), tsunamis, and active volcanoes such as Mount Pinatubo in the Philippines.

Wildlife is abundant and varied, but the two animals which best represent the continent—the panda and the tiger—are found nowhere else.

Bagan, in Myanmar, was once the capital of the First Myanmar Empire. It is one of the richest archeological sites in Southeast Asia.

GEORGIA

Georgia's decision not to join the Commonwealth of Independent States in 1991 after the breakup of the Soviet Union was based on political and interethnic differences, but also highlights the nation's independent spirit. A mountainous country, Georgia's landscape is dominated by lofty ranges (such as the Caucasus) and plateaus cut by deep river valleys. The swampy plains of Kolkhida fringe the Black Sea coast. The mountainous terrain produces a varied climate, generally cold in the mountains but almost subtropical in the Kolkhida

Lowlands. Much of the country is wooded, but the drier east has grassland. Wildlife includes bears and wolves.

Georgia's long history includes domination by the ancient Greeks and the Romans, while later coming under the influence of the Persians and the Ottoman Turks. Fragmented in the 18th century, the country was reunited in the 19th century under Russian rule; despite this, Georgia remained resistant to Russian influences. Violence and unrest marked the years following independence, and although progress toward stability has been achieved, there remain the unresolved issues over two breakaway regions—Abkhazia and South Ossetia—which are outside central government control.

Georgia produces tea, fruits, tobacco, and wines, as well as sugar beet and essential oils. The main livestock are sheep. Collectivization of agriculture had less impact in Georgia, so privately owned plots flourished. Rich mineral and energy resources include coal, natural gas, manganese, and other metals. Traditional industries include steelworking, engineering, and chemicals. Georgia's rich tradition of arts and culture can be seen in icon painting, metalwork, embroidered textiles, and carving. Georgia enjoys a high standard of healthcare and education.

NATIONAL DATA – GEORGIA

Land area	69,700 sq km (26,911sq mi)			

Climate		Temperatures		Annual
	Altitude m (ft)	January °C(°F)	July °C(°F)	precipitation mm (in)
Tbilisi	490 (1,608)	1 (34)	24 (75)	500 (19.7)

Major physical features highest point: Shkhara 5,201 m (17,063 ft); longest river: Kura (part) 1,514 km (941 mi)

Population (2006 est.) 4,661,473

Form of government multiparty republic with one legislative house

Armed forces army 7,042; navy 1,350; air force 1,350

Largest cities Tbilisi (capital - 1,026,874); Kutaisi (173,000); Batumi (115,806); Rustavi (105,393)

Official language Georgian

Ethnic composition Georgian 83.8%; Azeri 6.5%; Armenian 5.7%; Russian 1.5%; other 2.5%

Religious affiliations Orthodox Christian 83.9%; Muslim 9.9%; Armenian-Gregorian 3.9%; Catholic 0.8%; other 0.8%; none 0.7%

Currency 1 lari (GEL) = 100 tetri

Gross domestic product (2006) U.S. $17.79 billion

Gross domestic product per capita (2006) U.S. $3,800

Life expectancy at birth male 72.8 yr; female 79.87 yr

Major resources coal, natural gas, forests, hydropower, manganese, copper, citrus fruits, grapes/wine, sugar beet, livestock, vegetables

ARMENIA

The landlocked republic of Armenia lies to the south of the Caucasus. It also claims the Armenian-populated enclave of Nagorno-Karabakh—across its eastern frontier with Azerbaijan—a cause that has led to outbreaks of violence since the late 1980s. Armenia's landscape is dominated by the Little Caucasus, with its considerable peaks characterized by extinct volcanoes and high lava plateaus cut by deep ravines. The highest peak, Aragats, lies in the northwest. The climate is dry and continental. There are short winters and long hot summers on the plains, but it is much colder in the mountains. Steppe vegetation predominates at lower altitudes, where jackals and leopards are found. In the southeast there are oak forests, merging with beechwoods in the northeast. Animals here include squirrels and bears.

The people of Armenia are survivors of an ancient civilization that was once fought over by Mongols, Turks, and Persians. Later the area was a Soviet republic, but it joined the Commonwealth of Independent States in 1991 and became a member of the UN in 1992.

Sanahin Monastery, in the northern Tumanian district, is a fine example of medieval Armenian architecture.

Agriculture is the main source of income, especially in the Aras valley and around Yerevan. Crops include grapes, figs, and cereals. Sheep and cattle are reared on the mountains. The country industrialized fast in the second half of the 20th century, exploiting its reserves of minerals. Industries include engineering, and the country also exports textiles and alcoholic beverages. An earthquake in 1988 disrupted the economy greatly.

NATIONAL DATA – ARMENIA

Land area   28,400 sq km (10,965 sq mi)

Climate	Altitude m (ft)	Temperatures January °C(°F)	July °C(°F)	Annual precipitation mm (in)
Yerevan	990 (3,248)	-4 (25)	20 (68)	277 (10.9)

Major physical features   highest point: Aragats 4,090 m (13,418 ft); longest river: Aras (part) 914 km (568 mi); largest lake: Lake Sevan 1,360 sq km (525 sq mi)

Population   (2006 est.) 2,976,372

Form of government   multiparty republic with one legislative house

Armed forces   army 45,000; air force 3,160

Largest cities   Yerevan (capital – 1,086,174); Gyumri (151,450); Vanadzor (104,242)

Official language   Armenian

Ethnic composition   Armenian 97.9%; Yezidi (Kurd) 1.3%; Russian 0.5%; other 0.3%

Religious affiliations   Armenian Apostolic 94.7%; other Christian 4%; Yezidi (monotheist with elements of nature worship) 1.3%

Currency   1 dram (AMD) = 100 luma

Gross domestic product   (2006) U.S. $15.99 billion

Gross domestic product per capita   (2006) U.S. $5,400

Life expectancy at birth   male 68.25 yr; female 76.02 yr

Major resources   gold, copper, molybdenum, zinc, alumina, antimony, arsenic, barley, chromites, citrus fruits, cotton, figs, iron, limestone, livestock, magnesium, mercury, potatoes, pumice, silver, sugar beet, tobacco, wheat, wine/grapes

TURKEY

Turkey spans both Europe and Asia across the narrow straits of Bosporus and the Dardanelles. European Turkey lies north of the Sea of Marmara and shares borders with Bulgaria and Greece. Asian Turkey is larger and borders several Arab countries as well as Armenia and Georgia. Istanbul is strategically positioned at the entrance to the Black Sea, controlling a major shipping route.

NATIONAL DATA – TURKEY

Land area 770,760 sq km (297,592 sq mi)

Climate	Altitude m (ft)	Temperatures January °C(°F)	July °C(°F)	Annual precipitation mm (in)
Ankara	861 (2,825)	1 (34)	23 (73)	384 (15.1)
Izmir	28 (92)	9 (48)	28 (82)	686 (27)

Major physical features highest point: Ararat 5,165 m (16,945 ft); largest lake: Lake Van 3,675 sq km (1,419 sq mi); longest river: Kizil Irmak 1,150 km (715 mi); (Euphrates and Tigris also rise in Turkey)

Population (2006 est.) 70,413,958

Form of government multiparty republic with one legislative house

Armed forces army 402,000; navy 52,750; air force 60,100

Largest cities Istanbul (10,291,102); Ankara (capital – 3,641,931); Izmir (2,615,568); Bursa (1,504,817); Adana (1,294,460)

Official language Turkish

Ethnic composition Turkish 80%; Kurdish 20%

Religious affiliations Muslim 99.8% (mainly Sunni); other 0.2% (mainly Christians and Jews)

Currency 1 Turkish lira (YTL) = 100 kurus

Gross domestic product (2006) U.S. $6.27.2 billion

Gross domestic product per capita (2006) U.S. $8,900

Life expectancy at birth male 70.18 yr; female 75.18 yr

Major resources coal, iron ore, copper, chromium, antimony, mercury, gold, barite, borate, celestite (strontium), emery, feldspar, limestone, magnesite, marble, perlite, pumice, pyrites (sulfur), clay, cotton, tea, tobacco, wheat, barley, rice, sugar beet, olives, grapes/sultanas, figs, hazelnuts, tourism, hydropower

Geography

The European part of Turkey (called Thrace) has fertile rolling plains surrounded by low mountains. On the Asian side (much of which is known as Asia Minor), western Anatolia is crossed by mountain ridges cut by deep valleys. South of the central Anatolian plateau the Taurus Mountains flank the Mediterranean coast. Farther east, higher mountain ranges culminate in the massive cone of Mount Ararat, the highest peak in Turkey. To the southwest is Lake Van. Frequent earthquakes, plus geysers and other volcanic activity, are evidence that this is a tectonically active region.

Rainfall is highest along the Black Sea coast, where temperatures are high all year. The central plateaus of the interior are semiarid. Snow can be persistent in the eastern mountains. Thick scrubland characterizes the Mediterranean south and west of Turkey. Dense forest grows around the Black Sea area, while inland the drier terrain is covered mainly by steppe grassland. Animals such as bears and red deer are found in the forests, and flocks of flamingoes thrive on some of the lakes.

Society

Asia Minor has seen the rise and fall of many of the world's great empires. The Anatolian Empire, the Persian Empire, the Greek Empire, and then the Roman Empire successively took control of the region. From the 11th century Asia Minor was invaded by Turkish rulers. Osman I (1258–1326) is generally regarded as the

founder of the Ottoman state. In the 15th century the Ottomans took over Constantinople, renaming it Istanbul, and gained control of much of Asia Minor. Later rulers extended the empire's borders. By the 19th century the Ottoman empire had started to disintegrate, and defeat in the Balkan Wars of 1912-13 reduced European Turkey to its present size. In 1918 the empire was dismembered and the country was weak. Meanwhile, a revolutionary movement led by Mustafa Kemal (later known as Kemal Atatürk; 1881-1938) had set up government in Ankara. As Turkey's first president, he transformed and Westernized Turkish society and laid the foundations for a strong modern nation.

Economy

The economy has been hampered by the need to import some fuel and food. Local coal is available, but petroleum needs to be imported. Up to half the country's energy comes from hydroelectric power. A major hydroelectric power and irrigation program, the Great Anatolian Project, is nearing completion on the headwaters of the Tigris and Euphrates Rivers—22 dams and 19 power stations are being constructed. Programs such as this are planned to increase Turkey's energy production by 70 percent. Irrigation in the coastal lowlands enables the country to produce the largest crops of hazelnuts and sultanas in the world. These and other cash crops such as cotton, tea, and tobacco are vital for the export trade.

A DIFFICULT DIPLOMATIC PATH

Turkey's unusual geographical location, as well as its foreign policy ambitions, cause difficult problems. In 1974 Turkey invaded—and still occupies—the northern part of Cyprus, leading to a long-running dispute with Greece. This unresolved issue is one of several factors serving to hinder Turkey's application to join the EU. In 1991 Turkey, a member of NATO, imposed sanctions during the 1991 Gulf War, which damaged its economy. It was also obliged to take in Iraqi Kurdish refugees, despite having to deal with unrest among the Kurdish population in its own eastern provinces.

Iron, aluminum, and copper ores supply raw materials for industry. The textile industry, producing yarn, fabric, and rugs, accounts for about 40 percent of exports. Money sent home from Turks working in places such as Germany is also an important contribution to the economy. However, the largest sector of the economy is now tourism, which is especially important around the western coastal resorts.

Turkey has the best-developed road and railroad systems in the Middle East. The state airline serves major international and domestic airports. Healthcare is free for the poor, but housing is in short supply.

The Euphrates Valley in Turkey. The longest river in western Asia, the Euphrates River flows for 1,096 km (680 mi) through Turkey.

AZERBAIJAN

Azerbaijan occupies the southeast corner of Transcaucasia. Its territories include the autonomous oblast region of Nagorno-Karabakh—which is also claimed by Armenia—and the autonomous republic of Nakhichevan. The country rejoined the Commonwealth of Independent States in 1993, but is also forging links with Turkey. The north of the country is dominated by the Great Caucasus Mountains that extend to Baku. In the foothills, the Kura River valley drops southeastward

NATIONAL DATA – AZERBAIJAN

Land area	86,100 sq km (33,243 sq mi)
Climate	humid subtropical to dry continental
Major physical features	highest point: Bazardyuze 4,480 m (14,698 ft); lowest point: Caspian Sea –28 m (–92 ft); longest river: Kura (part) 1,510 km (940 mi)
Population	(2006 est.) 7,961,619
Form of government	multiparty republic with one legislative house
Armed forces	army 56,840; navy 2,000; air force 7,900
Largest cities	Baku (capital – 1,118,904); Gäncä (304,472); Sumgayit (268,336)
Official language	Azerbaijani
Ethnic composition	Azeri 90.6%; Dagestani 2.2%; Russian 1.8%; Armenian 1.5%; other 3.9%
Religious affiliations	Muslim 93.4%; Russian Orthodox 2.5%; Armenian Orthodox 2.3%; other 1.8%
Currency	1 Azerbaijani manat (AZM) = 100 gopiks
Gross domestic product	(2006) U.S. $58.1 billion
Gross domestic product per capita	(2006) U.S. $7,300
Life expectancy at birth	male 59.78 yr; female 68.13 yr
Major resources	petroleum, natural gas, iron ore, nonferrous metals, alumina, cotton, tobacco, fruit, fisheries

A shop displaying carpets and other items in the capital and chief port, Baku, situated on the eastern promontory of Azerbaijan.

onto a broad flood plain. Nakhichevan and regions of west and south Azerbaijan are also mountainous. The climate ranges from dry and subtropical in the lowlands to snowy in the mountains and wetter in the south. The vegetation varies from grassland to forests and marshes.

Azerbaijan has little arable land, but is a major producer of cotton, tobacco, and fruit. The Caspian Sea is an important source of fish, but pollution threatens this resource. Baku was a major oil producer during the Soviet era. There has since been Western investment in the oil industry, which now accounts for 90 percent of the country's exports. The war with Armenia over the territory of Nagorno-Karabakh has damaged the economy, however.

SYRIA

Syria's Mediterranean seaboard is one of the country's most fertile and densely populated regions. Inland are the mountains of the Jebel Ansariye. Across the mountains the Asi River flows through the deep Ghab Depression. Mountains continue along the Lebanese border as far as the Golan Heights, occupied by Israel. Extending north and east from the mountains is a broad, semiarid plateau that becomes the Syrian Desert. The climate is generally hot and dry in summer and mild in winter. According to location, vegetation ranges from scrub and dry grassland to maquis and forests. Wildlife includes jerboas, gazelles, lizards, boars, wolves, and various species of birds.

Syria's frontiers were drawn up at the end of World War I by the Allies. Since then it has played a leading role in Middle Eastern politics, but the government's hardline Arab nationalism has led Syria into frequent conflicts with its neighbors, especially Israel. The Syrian economy is burdened by huge military spending. It is still largely agriculturally based, despite modernization since World War II. Modest petroleum reserves provide most export revenue. Agriculture is mainly confined to the coast and along the Asi and Euphrates Rivers. Cotton is the chief cash crop. Sheep, goats, and camels are reared on pastures irrigated by artificial terraces. Hydroelectric stations on the Euphrates, supplemented with oil-fired thermal stations, supply electricity. Industries include textiles, food processing, and engineering. Road and railroad networks are well developed, but social infrastructures are generally poor.

The village of Maalula, an ancient settlement perched on the Kalamun Mountains about 50 km (30 mi) from Damascus.

NATIONAL DATA – SYRIA

Land area 184,050sq km (71,062 sq mi)

Climate	Altitude m (ft)	Temperatures January °C(°F)	July °C(°F)	Annual precipitation mm (in)
Damascus	720 (2,362)	7 (45)	27 (81)	133 (5.2)

Major physical features highest point: Mount Hermon 2,814 m (9,232 ft); longest river: Euphrates (part) 3,596 km (2,235 mi)

Population (2006 est.) 18,881,361

Form of government multiparty republic with one legislative house

Armed forces army 200,000; navy 7,600; air force 40,000

Largest cities Aleppo (1,649,694); Damascus (capital – 1,592,206); Homs (822,440); Hama (495,390)

Official language Arabic

Ethnic composition Arab 90.3%; Kurds, Armenians, and other 9.7%

Religious affiliations Sunni Muslim 74%; Alawite, Druze, and other Muslim sects 16%; Christian (various sects) 10%; Jewish (communities in Damascus, Al Qamishli, and Aleppo)

Currency 1 Syrian pound (SYP) = 100 piastres

Gross domestic product (2006) U.S. $75.1 billion

Gross domestic product per capita (2006) U.S. $4,00

Life expectancy at birth male 69.01 yr; female 71.7 yr

Major resources petroleum, phosphates, chrome and manganese ores, asphalt, iron ore, rock salt, marble, gypsum, hydropower, barley, cattle, cotton, fruit, goats, natural gas, potatoes, sheep, sugar beet, vegetables, wheat

ISRAEL

The people of Israel have historic links with the region that go back more than 3,000 years. However, the Jewish claims to the land conflict with those of the Palestinian Arabs, whose historical ties are no less ancient. Jews make up the majority of the population, more than half of whom are now Israeli-born.

NATIONAL DATA – ISRAEL

Land area 20,330 sq km (7,849 sq mi)

Climate	Altitude m (ft)	Temperatures January °C(°F)	July °C(°F)	Annual precipitation mm (in)
Jerusalem	757 (2,484)	9 (48)	24 (75)	544 (21.4)

Major physical features highest point: Mount Meron 1,125 m (3,962 ft); lowest point: Dead Sea –418 m (-1,371 ft); longest river: Jordan (part) 320 km (200 mi)

Population (2006 est.) 6,352,117

Form of government multiparty republic with one legislative house

Armed forces army 125,000; navy 7,600; air force 35,000

Largest cities Jerusalem (capital – 743,512); Tel Aviv-Jaffa (388,288); Haifa (265,796)

Official languages Hebrew, Arabic

Ethnic composition Jewish 76.4% (Europe/America-born 22.6%; Israel-born 67.1%; Africa-born 5.9%; Asia-born 4.2%); non-Jewish 23.6% (mainly arab)

Religious affiliations Jewish 76.4%; Muslim 16%; Arab Christians 1.7%; other Christian 0.4%; Druze 1.6%; unspecified 3.9%

Currency 1 new Israeli shekel (ILS) = 100 agorot

Gross domestic product (2006) U.S. $166.3 billion

Gross domestic product per capita (2006) U.S. $26,200

Life expectancy at birth male 77.33 yr; female 81.7 yr

Major resources timber, potash, copper ore, natural gas, phosphate rock, magnesium bromide, clays, sand, tourism, citrus fruit, vegetables, cotton, groundnuts (peanuts), diamond processing, crude oil, figs, grapes, livestock, olives, sugar beet, vegetables, wheat

Geography

Israel is bounded by the Mediterranean Sea to the west, Lebanon to the north, Syria to the northeast, Jordan to the east, and Egypt to the southwest. The country can be divided into four main areas: the densely populated fertile strip of Mediterranean coastal plains; the central hills that extend from Galilee in the north to Judea in the center; the Great Rift Valley running the length of the eastern borders to the Gulf of Aqaba; and the Negev Desert in the south. The Jordan River flows south into the Dead Sea; the latter is renowned for being the world's saltiest body of water (at 25 percent salinity) and also the lowest point on Earth's surface at 418 m (1,371 ft) below the Mediterranean, and falling.

Heavy rain falls in the cooler northern highlands in winter, but very little falls in the south. Summers are hot and dry. Most of the original evergreen forests have been cleared over the centuries, but there has been widespread reforestation, with conifers and eucalyptus and citrus trees being planted. The main form of vegetation is scrub, including Mediterranean maquis in the central hills. Nature reserves have been set up

to preserve the varied wildlife, which includes caracals, cheetahs, leopards, hyraxes, addaxes, ibex, geckos, and turtles such as the hawksbill turtle.

Society

The hinterland of Palestine is of great significance, not only for Jews throughout the world but also for Christians and Muslims. Jerusalem is a holy city for all three religions. Modern Israel occupies approximately three-quarters of the area known as Palestine. The Bible (the Jewish Torah) describes how nomadic Hebrew peoples escaped from Egyptian captivity to settle in the land of the Canaanites (from whom the modern Palestinian Arabs claim descent). By 400 B.C. Palestine was under Roman rule, and most Jews were scattered.

By the time Palestine was conquered by Muslim Arabs in the 7th century, Jews were a small part of a largely Christian kingdom. The Ottoman Turks then ruled the region for some 400 years. The state of Israel, declared in 1948, made territorial gains in wars with Arab neighbors. These included the Gaza Strip, the West Bank of the Jordan River, and the Golan Heights on the

Temple Mount in Jerusalem, showing the Western (Wailing) Wall and the golden Dome of the Rock.

Syrian border. Peace accords have since led to progressive Israeli withdrawals and expansion of Palestinian self-rule, but no final peace agreement has been achieved, and unrest continues.

Economy

Israel's economic growth and stability have been greatly helped by financial support from the United States. and by Jewish communities around the world. At the same time, huge economic problems arise from the need to spend a large part of the budget on defense, and also by Israel's inability to trade with any of its near neighbors—all of which are Arab countries. Israel pioneered the cooperative agricultural settlements—*kibbutzim* and *moshavim*—and improved the efficiency of the land through irrigation and mechanization, but the kibbutz system has almost been disbanded. Crops include citrus fruits (a major export), cotton, and peanuts. The Dead Sea yields valuable bromides and magnesium salts, and some petroleum is extracted.

Food processing is the principal manufacturing activity but textiles, chemicals, and electronics are important, along with armaments. Diamond cutting is a major source of foreign currency, and tourism also brings income from foreigners. The road and railroad networks are well developed, and there are major ports at Elat on the Gulf of Aqaba and on the Mediterranean. Literacy, health, and housing standards tend to be high, especially among the Jewish population.

WEST BANK, GAZA STRIP

An agreement signed between Israel and the PLO (Palestine Liberation Organization) in 1993 began the process of providing for Palestinian self-government in the Gaza Strip and the West Bank. It was also agreed that Israel would retain responsibility for security and for Israeli citizens during the transitional period. In 2000 negotiations to determine the permanent status of the region were halted as a result of uprisings. In 2003 the United States, the EU, the UN, and Russia laid out a "roadmap" to a final settlement, based on terms being agreed between Israel and a democratic Palestine. The final date for a permanent status agreement has been postponed indefinitely because of continuing violence and internal squabbles. In 2005 Israel withdrew all of its settlers, soldiers, and military equipment from the Gaza Strip and several West Bank settlements, but it still controls access to the Gaza Strip.

The economy of the region is hampered by limited land access, a high population density, and the uncertain political and military situation—one outcome of which was the destruction of much of the industrial infrastructure during clashes. Half the labor force is unemployed, including many who formerly worked in Israel, and poverty is rife. Agriculture occupies about 12 percent of the workforce, who grow mainly olives, fruit, and vegetables, and rear cattle for beef and dairy products. Industry employs 18 percent of the workforce; much of this involves small family businesses producing items such as textiles, soap, and olive wood carvings.

The ruins of Qumran, an ancient monastery. In 1947 a boy discovered a cave nearby containing more than 500 manuscripts, now known as the Dead Sea Scrolls. The texts are thought to be the only known surviving Biblical documents written before 100 A.D.

NATIONAL DATA – WEST BANK, GAZA STRIP

Land area   West Bank 5,640 sq km (2,178 sq mi); Gaza Strip 360 sq km (139 sq mi)

Climate   West Bank warm to hot summers, cool to mild winters; Gaza Strip mild winters, dry and warm to hot summers

Major physical features   West Bank - highest point Tall Asur 1,022 m (3,353 ft), lowest point Dead Sea –418 m (–1,371 ft); Gaza Strip - highest point: Abu 'Awdah 105 m (345 ft)

Population   (2006 est.) West Bank 2,460,492; Gaza Strip 1,428,757

Form of government   Palestinian Authority (PA) is an interim administrative organization that nominally governs parts of the West Bank and the Gaza Strip. The Palestinian Legislative Council (PLC) is an elected body of 132 representatives and acts as a parliament

Armed forces   PA is not permitted conventional military forces

Largest city   Gaza City 400,000

Official languages   Arabic, Hebrew, English

Religious affiliations   West Bank - Muslim 75%; Jewish 17%; other 8%; Gaza - Muslim 98.7%; Christian 0.7%; Jewish 0.6%

Currency   1 new Israeli shekel (ILS) = 100 agorot

Gross domestic product   (2003) U.S. $2.568 billion

Gross domestic product per capita   (2003) West Bank U.S. $1,100; Gaza U.S. $600

Life expectancy at birth   male 71.08 yr; female 74.24

Major resources   olives, citrus fruit, vegetables, beef, dairy products, limestone, natural gas

LEBANON

Lebanon is bordered by Israel and Syria. The latter has played a leading role in Lebanon's affairs, only recently withdrawing its troops. Lebanon is a deeply divided nation struggling to rebuild its economy and preserve a fragile stability. The long civil war that ended in 1991 devastated the economy and ruined the capital, Beirut. The country's infrastructure was damaged again in 2006 during a short but intense conflict with Israel.

NATIONAL DATA – LEBANON

Land area	10,230 sq km (3,950 sq mi)			
Climate		**Temperatures**		**Annual**
	Altitude m (ft)	January °C(°F)	July °C(°F)	precipitation mm (in)
Beirut	34 (112)	13 (55)	25 (77)	873 (34.4)

Major physical features	highest point: Qurnat as Sawda 3,088 m (10,131 ft); longest river: Litani 145 km (90 mi)
Population	(2006 est.) 3,874,050
Form of government	republic with one legislative house and no party system
Armed forces	army 70,000; navy 1,100; air force 1,000
Largest cities	Beirut (capital – 1,295,078); Tripoli (237,909)
Official language	Arabic
Ethnic composition	Arab 95%; Armenian 4%; other 1%
Religious affiliations	Muslim 59.7% (Shi'a, Sunni, Druze, Isma'ilite, Alawite or Nusayri); Christian 39% (Maronite Catholic, Greek Orthodox, Melkite Catholic, Armenian Orthodox, Syrian Catholic, Armenian Catholic, Syrian Orthodox, Roman Catholic, Chaldean, Assyrian, Copt, Protestant); other 1.3%
Currency	1 Lebanese pound (LBP) = 100 piastres
Gross domestic product	(2006) U.S. $21.45 billion
Gross domestic product per capita	(2006) U.S. $5,500
Life expectancy at birth	male 70.41 yr; female 75.48 yr
Major resources	limestone, iron ore, salt, water-surplus state in a water-deficit region, grapes, citrus fruits, olives, tobacco, apples, cotton, goats, potatoes, sheep, sugar beet, wheat, hydroelectric power

A view of Beirut. The city, devastated by the long civil war, is the principal port, as well as the location of the airport.

The Lebanese Mountains rise from the narrow coastal plain, culminating in Qurnet es Sauda, before falling away south to the Galilee hills in Israel. East of the mountains the fertile Bekáa valley separates the Lebanon Mountains from the Hermon ranges along the Syrian border. Summers are hot and dry, while winters are mild and wet. Shrubs, oak, cypress, fir, and juniper are the main vegetation, with protected stands of Lebanon's cedar trees in the northern mountains.

Decades of conflict left the once-prosperous economy in ruins. Lebanon lost most of its international banking, although this has largely recovered. Agriculture is mostly confined to the coast and the Bekáa valley. Oil refining and food processing are the chief industries, but tourism is slowing reviving. Many Lebanese have left to work abroad, and their place has been filled by workers from other Arab countries. Housing is in short supply, and healthcare is centered on urban areas.

JORDAN

Jordan is a small Arab kingdom with access to the Red Sea and beyond via a narrow coastline in the far southwest. Until the Arab–Israeli War of 1967 Jordan held the West Bank area of the Jordan River, which included the Old City of Jerusalem. Jordan formally renounced claim to this territory in 1988. This area is now slowly being ceded to the Palestinians by Israel.

Geography

The country's western border with Israel runs along the bottom of the Ghor Depression—a deep rift valley that contains the Dead Sea, the lowest point on Earth's surface. The Dead Sea is fed from the north by the

NATIONAL DATA – JORDAN

Land area 91,971 sq km (35,510 sq mi)

Climate		Temperatures		Annual
	Altitude m (ft)	January °C(°F)	July °C(°F)	precipitation mm (in)
Amman	771 (2,529)	8 (46)	25 (77)	273 (10.7)

Major physical features highest point: Jebel Ramm 1,754 m (5,755 ft); lowest point: Dead Sea –418 m (–1,371 ft); longest river: Jordan (part) 320 km (200 mi)

Population (2006 est.) 5,906,760

Form of government multiparty constitutional monarchy with two legislative houses

Armed forces army 85,000; navy 500; air force 15,000

Largest cities Amman (capital - 1,331,028); Zarqa (494,655); Irbid (327,543)

Official language Arabic

Ethnic composition Arab 98%; Circassian 1%; Armenian 1%

Official religion Islam

Religious affiliations Sunni Muslim 92%; Christian 6% (mainly Greek Orthodox, but some Greek and Roman Catholics, Syrian Orthodox, Coptic Orthodox, Armenian Orthodox, and Protestants); other 2% (small Shi'a Muslim and Druze populations)

Currency 1 Jordanian dinar (JOD) = 1,000 fils

Gross domestic product (2006) U.S. $28.89 billion

Gross domestic product per capita (2006) U.S. $4,900

Life expectancy at birth male 75.9 yr; female 81.05 yr

Major resources phosphates, potash, shale oil, olives, citrus fruits, grapes, tourism, olive oil, vegetables, wheat

Jordan River and from the south by the Wadi Araba. Mountains overlook the valley, and beyond them lie the barren plateaus and basins of the great North Arabian Desert, which merges in the northeast with the rolling lands of the Syrian Desert. Jordan is an arid country, although the western highlands receive some rainfall in the cooler winter season. In summer it is hot everywhere except on the highest slopes. Between April and October there is little rainfall anywhere, and there are frequently water shortages as a result.

Jordan's vegetation ranges from Mediterranean plants in the mountains to sagebrush, grasses, and scattered shrubs in the dry steppes. A few hardy plant species grow in the eastern deserts, especially in basins irrigated by seasonal streams flowing down from the nearby mountains.

Society

From 800 B.C. to the 7th century A.D. the part of the Middle East now called Jordan was ruled successively by Assyrians, Babylonians, Persians, Greeks, Romans, and Muslim Arabs. From the 16th century the region became an imperial province of the Ottoman Turks, until they were driven out in an Arab rebellion during World War I. In 1921 Britain separated out the semi-autonomous region of Transjordan, but it was a British protectorate until independence in 1946. It took the name of Jordan in 1950. In 1952 King Hussein ibn-Talal (1935–99) inherited the throne. Raids on Israel by Palestinians living in Jordanian land provoked fierce reprisals.

In 1967 Jordan joined Arab neighbors in a war against Israel; as a result, it lost all Palestinian territories west of the Jordan River. In the ensuing years Hussein used his skills to juggle the competing influences from the United States, the Soviet Union, Britain, other Arab nations, and a large internal Palestinian population. In 1994 he signed a peace treaty with Israel. The vast majority of Jordan's inhabitants are Arabic-speaking Arabs. Over half the population are Palestinians, many of whom are cared for by the UN.

The remains of Petra, an ancient city cut into the sandstone rock. Jordan's best-known tourist attraction, it was founded by the Edomite peoples in about 1000 B.C.

Economy

The loss of agricultural land and tourist revenue from the West Bank in 1967 impacted severely on the economy, and Jordan is now greatly dependent on foreign grants and loans. Natural resources are few, and the country imports half of its food requirements. Irrigation in parts of the Jordan valley and adjoining mountain valleys has made farming possible. Although the spread of agriculture has reduced the amount of grazing land available to livestock, some sheep and goats are reared for meat and milk. Some fishing takes place in the Gulf of Aqaba, and reforestation in the eastern highlands has increased forestry activity.

The discovery of phosphate and potash reserves have boosted the country's industrial development. Manufactured goods include foodstuffs, textiles, chemicals, cement, and electrical goods. Imported oil is the main source of energy. Jordan has various ancient archaeological sites, such as Petra, which attract tourists.

A well-developed system of roads exists, and the Hejaz railroad runs north–south between the Syrian and Saudi borders through the capital, Amman. There is also a branch line to the port of Aqaba. International airports are located at Amman and Aqaba. Healthcare, which is government funded, is available only in the cities. Housing, sanitation, and food are often inadequate, with diseases such as typhoid, hepatitis, and dysentery not fully under control. Literacy levels among women remain low.

JORDAN'S "NEW" CAPITAL CITY

Unlike the capital cities of other Arab nations, Jordan's capital, Amman, is a new town. Sited on seven hills northeast of the Dead Sea, it has been constructed almost completely since the 1880s over the ruins of the ancient Roman city of Philadelphia. As well as being the administrative center of the country, Amman is the hub for business, road, railroad, and air transportation communications. Despite its relative modernity, it is still possible to get lost in the city's maze of narrow, twisting streets. The city's infrastructure is now severely strained by the presence of thousands of Palestinian refugees.

IRAQ

Iraq, an Arab republic on the Persian Gulf, was the site of the ancient civilizations of Babylonia and Assyria. More recently, Iraq has been notable for its invasion of neighboring countries, carrying out genocide against its own Kurdish population, and for being invaded itself by U.S.-led coalition forces. Despite attempts by the new, freely elected Iraqi government to create a democratic and stable country, it faces violence and insurgency.

NATIONAL DATA - IRAQ

Land area	432,162 sq km (166,859 sq mi)			

Climate	Altitude m (ft)	Temperatures January °C(°F)	July °C(°F)	Annual precipitation mm (in)
Baghdad	34 (112)	9 (48)	35 (95)	155 (6.1)

Major physical features highest point: Huji Ibrahim 3,904 m (12,808 ft); longest river: Euphrates (part) 3,596 km (2,235 mi)

Population (2006 est.) 26,783,383

Form of government parliamentary democracy with one legislative house

Armed forces army 105,700; navy 800; air force 500

Largest cities Baghdad (capital - 5,831,541); Mosul (2,220,624); Basra (2,271,544); Irbil (993,468); Sulaimaniyah (773,496); Kirkuk (610,954); An Najaf (502,400)

Ethnic composition Arab 75%–80%; Kurdish 15%–20%; Turkoman, Assyrian or other 5%

Official religion Islam

Religious affiliations Muslim 97% (Shi'a 60%–65%; Sunni 32%–37%); Christian or other 3%

Currency 1 New Iraqi dinar (NID) = 20 dirhams = 1,000 fils

Gross domestic product (2005) U.S. $94.1 billion

Gross domestic product per capita (2006) U.S. $1,900

Life expectancy at birth male 67.76 yr; female 70.31 yr

Major resources petroleum, natural gas, phosphates, sulphur, camels, cattle, cereals, cotton, goats, sheep, tomatoes

Geography

Southwestern Iraq consists of desert, and the northeast is mountainous. Between is the fertile Tigris–Euphrates river basin; the rivers meet to form a vast swamp on their route to the Persian Gulf. Toward the center of the country the land rises through steppeland northwest of Baghdad. In the far north is higher ground, while northeast of the Tigris the land rises to high mountains on the Turkish and Iranian borders. Summers are hot and humid in the Tigris–Euphrates basin; winters are cooler. Northeast Iraq is generally cooler, with more rain. The steppe vegetation of the north and east gives way to thorny tamarisks and salt-resistant plants in the south and west. Willows and poplars line riverbanks, while sedges and reeds grow in the marshlands. Migrant birds flock to the swamps and lakes in winter.

The excavated and restored ziggurat at Ur, a monument at the ancient Sumerian city about 300 km (186 mi) from Baghdad.

Society

Mesopotamia, the fertile land between the Tigris and Euphrates, was the cradle of ancient civilization. The empires of Persia, Macedonia, Greece, Rome, and Britain all controlled the region at some time. Iraq gained independence in 1932. Saddam Hussein (1937–2006) became president in 1979. Invasion of Iran over control of the strategic Shatt-el-Arab waterway followed in 1980, but hopes of a quick victory were dashed, and the bloody and costly conflict lasted until 1989.

In 1990 Saddam invaded Kuwait to seize the oilfields but was quickly driven out by an international force. The UN imposed strict economic sanctions on Iraq, but more clashes with UN forces ensued. Following Iraq's non-compliance over UN resolutions concerning the issue of weapons of mass destruction, a U.S.-led invasion took place in 2003, toppling Saddam's regime and placing him and many others on trial. Saddam was convicted of crimes against humanity and was executed in 2006. Coalition forces remain in Iraq, helping restore the damaged infrastructure and supporting the new government, but increasing violence between Shi'ite and Sunni Muslims, as well as attacks on Coalition forces by Arab terrorist groups, remain a huge problem.

Economy

Oil is the mainstay of the Iraqi economy, which has in the past yielded 95 percent of foreign earnings. Iraq's invasion of Kuwait, the ensuing economic sanctions, and the infrastructure damage caused by the 1991 Gulf War, dramatically reduced oil production, however. The aftermath of the 2003 invasion of Iraq by the U.S.-led coalition included attacks on oil installations and other targets by insurgents, which resulted in further problems. The military victory of the coalition in 2003 also caused a shutdown of much of the country's economic administrative structure. Agriculture was also affected by sanctions. Vegetables and cereals are the most important crops, but trade was disrupted. About one-tenth of the land area provides grazing for livestock.

The transportation network has also suffered during the violence, as has the social infrastructure.

A LOST WAY OF LIFE

The marshy lowlands of southern Iraq have been home to the Marsh Arabs for thousands of years. These seminomadic peoples have herded water buffalo and hunted wildfowl, building elaborately constructed houses supported by arches woven from reeds. This way of life has long been under threat, and Saddam Hussein's destructive drainage program of the 1990s was designed to reclaim land and pursue rebels hiding from his government. It also forced most of the Marsh Arabs from their traditional homelands into refugee camps. Only a small percentage of the marshes remain.

SAUDI ARABIA

Saudi Arabia is named for the royal dynasty of Sa'ud, which has ruled the country since 1932. This huge desert kingdom occupies most of the Arabian Peninsula. In the 1930s the discovery of oil along the Persian Gulf coast of Saudi Arabia brought vast wealth to the country. It is estimated that Saudi Arabia has about one-quarter of the world's oil reserves. Money from oil has enabled the country to modernize greatly, but it still follows traditional Islamic laws.

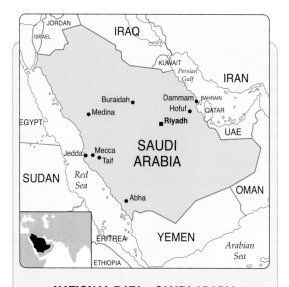

NATIONAL DATA – SAUDI ARABIA

Land area	2,149,690 sq km (830,000 sq mi)			

Climate	Altitude m (ft)	Temperatures January °C(°F)	July °C(°F)	Annual precipitation mm (in)
Riyadh	609 (1,998)	14 (58)	35 (95)	113 (4.4)

Major physical features highest point: Jabal Sawda 3,133 m (10,279 ft)

Population (2006 est.) 27,019,731

Form of government absolute monarchy

Armed forces army 75,000; navy 15,500; air force 18,000

Largest cities Riyadh (capital – 4,453,447); Jedda (3,002,839); Mecca (1,383,707)

Official language Arabic

Ethnic composition Saudi 82.0%; Yemeni 9.6%; other Arabs 3.4%; others 5.0%

Religious affiliations Muslim 96.7%; Christian 2.9%; others 0.4%

Currency 1 Saudi riyal (SAR) = 100 hallalah

Gross domestic product (2006) U.S. $374 billion

Gross domestic product per capita (2006) U.S. $13,800

Life expectancy at birth male 73.66 yr; female 77.78 yr

Major resources petroleum, natural gas, iron ore, gold, copper, wheat, dates, bananas, coffee, alfalfa, cattle, goats, camels, grapes, poultry, sheep, sorghum, watermelons

Geography

The Arabian Peninsula is largely a vast plateau. To the west it forms a steep escarpment parallel to the Red Sea coast, but in the northwest there is almost no coastal plain. The highest peaks are in the Asir Highlands in the southwest. East of the escarpment the barren plateau meets the waters of the Gulf, whose shores are lined with swamps and salt flats. The plateau is largely sandy desert, with areas of volcanic rock. A huge swath of desert known as the Empty Quarter occupies the whole of the south. The country has no permanent rivers; the Empty Quarter can go without rain for 10 years at a time. Other places experience downpours from time to time. Inland winters are cool, often with frost at night, but in summer temperatures can soar to 48°C (120°F).

In most parts vegetation consists of herbs and shrubs, with date palms in scattered oases. The Arabian oryx has been hunted almost to extinction, and the Arabian tahr and some birds of prey are endangered. Wild cats, desert-dwelling sandgrouse, and burrowing rodents such as jerboas, reptiles, and insects are common, and the Red Sea coral reefs teem with life.

Society

In 622 A.D. Muhammad (c.570–632), a merchant from Mecca, founded the religion of Islam at Medina. At the time of his death all Arabia was under the sway of Islam. By the 19th century the Arabian Peninsula was fragmented, and it fell to Ibn Sa'ud (c.1880–1953) to reunite the lands. In 1904 he regained Saudi rule in the region of Najd, and in 1924 he invaded the British protectorate of Hejaz, fulfilling his aim of taking Mecca and Medina. Three years later the British acknowledged his kingship over Najd and Hejaz, which he formally united in 1932 to form the Kingdom of Saudi Arabia. The country was neutral in World War II, but when Iraq invaded Kuwait in 1990 it allowed Western and Arab forces to deploy in its country in readiness for the liberation of Kuwait the following year.

Economy

The Saudi economy is based on petroleum exploitation— yielding 95 percent of export earnings in the past—and revenues from this finance heavy spending elsewhere.

Nevertheless, the government is aware that the oil boom is declining, and that revenues from oil may not sustain past levels of spending. Other concerns are the growing population and the depletion of aquifers, upon which water resources are founded. Huge government subsidies have helped produce surplus wheat for export, but two-thirds of all food is imported. Major crops include cereals, bananas, dates, and coffee. Sheep, goats, and camels are herded by nomads.

Saudi Arabia possesses significant quantities of natural gas and metal ores and enormous oil deposits. Manufacturing industries produce petrochemicals, fertilizers, and rolled steel. Wide-ranging welfare services are available for all citizens and visitors. Healthcare is good in cities, but in rural areas diseases such as malaria are common. Literacy levels are generally low; much of the workforce is provided by foreign workers.

The Great Mosque at Mecca. Many pilgrims come to worship at Mecca, the birthplace of Muhammad, and Islam's most holy city.

THE DESERT MONARCHY

The Saudi king, whose official title is Custodian of the Two Holy Mosques (at Mecca and Medina), rules as absolute monarch. His heir and deputy, the crown prince, is selected from the Sa'ud family by its leading members in consultation with the supreme religious council. The king governs according to Islamic law, choosing ministers, many of whom are Sa'uds. Islam is strictly enforced and affects every aspect of Saudi life. Violent unrest by opponents of the Saudi dynasty, and against Western interests in the country, has led to some concessions being granted by the government.

YEMEN

Yemen lies on the tip of the Arabian Peninsula. The landscape ranges from fertile highlands in the north to an arid coast and eastern region. In most places the climate is hot and dry. Three-quarters of the population live in rural areas, and the country's culture is based on traditional Islamic values. More than half the workforce is engaged in agriculture—mainly of the subsistence variety. Petroleum is the chief mineral resource, but despite this Yemen remains a poor country. Many Yemenis work abroad and send money home.

NATIONAL DATA - YEMEN

Land area	527,970 sq km (203,850 sq mi)			

Climate		Temperatures		Annual
	Altitude m (ft)	January °C(°F)	July °C(°F)	precipitation mm (in)
Aden	7 (23)	25 (77)	31 (88)	47 (1.8)

Major physical features	highest point: Jabal an-Nabi Shu'ayb 3,666 m (12,028 ft)

Population	(2006 est.) 21,456,188

Form of government	multiparty republic with one legislative house

Armed forces	army 60,000; navy 1,700; air force 5,000

Largest cities	San'a (capital – 2,015,515); Tai'zz (729,583); al-Hudaydah (713,458); Aden (646,180)

Official language	Arabic

Ethnic composition	Arab 92%; Afro-Arab 3%; Indian 3%; others 2%

Religious affiliations	Sunni Muslim 53.0%; Shi'ite Muslim 46.9%; others 0.1%

Currency	1 Yemeni rial (YER) = 100 fils

Gross domestic product	(2006) U.S. $20.38 billion

Gross domestic product per capita	(2006) U.S. $900

Life expectancy at birth	male 60.23 yr; female 64.11 yr

Major resources	petroleum, natural gas, rock salt, marble, coal, gold, lead, nickel, copper, cotton, coffee, hides and skins, fisheries, fruit, millet, sesame, sorghum, sugarcane, wheat

OMAN

In ancient times this part of the Arabian Peninsula was green and fertile, but now much is desert. Oman established strong links with Britain in the late 18th century and retained them after it ceased to be a British protectorate in 1951. Fishing and subsistence agriculture provide a living for local people, but the country's wealth comes from petroleum, which has also helped create manufacturing industries. Tourism, aimed at attracting Gulf Arabs, is also being developed.

NATIONAL DATA - OMAN

Land area	212,460 sq km (82,031 sq mi)			

Climate		Temperatures		Annual
	Altitude m (ft)	January °C(°F)	July °C(°F)	precipitation mm (in)
Muscat	5 (16)	22 (72)	34 (93)	98 (3.8)

Major physical features	highest point: Jabal Akhdar 3,074 m (10,086 ft)

Population	(2006 est.) 3,102,229

Form of government	monarchy with one appointed council

Armed forces	army 25,000; navy 4,200; air force 4,100

Capital city	Muscat (252,864)

Ethnic composition	Omani Arab 73%; Indian 13%; Pakistani 7%; Egyptian 2%; others 5%

Official religion	Islam

Religious affiliations	Muslim 88%; Hindu 7%; Christian 4%; others 1%

Currency	1 Omani rial (OMR) = 1,000 baiza

Gross domestic product	(2006) U.S. $43.88 billion

Gross domestic product per capita	(2006) U.S. $14,100

Life expectancy at birth	male 71.14 yr; female 75.72 yr

Major resources	petroleum, copper, asbestos, marble, limestone, chromium, gypsum, natural gas, fisheries, alfalfa, bananas, coconuts, dates, fruit, vegetables, wheat, tourism

UNITED ARAB EMIRATES

The United Arab Emirates is a federation of seven states ruled by emirs. The landscape is mainly sandy and lowlying, apart from the coastal salt flats and a range of mountains in the east. The climate is hot and dry all year. Only a tiny part of the land is suitable for agriculture, and most of the wealth comes from petroleum reserves and various manufacturing and service industries. Dubai has a thriving tourist industry.

NATIONAL DATA – UNITED ARAB EMIRATES

Land area 83,600 sq km (32,280 sq mi)

Climate	Altitude m (ft)	Temperatures January °C(°F)	July °C(°F)	Annual precipitation mm (in)
Abu Dhabi	5 (16)	18 (64)	35 (95)	798 (88.9)

Major physical features highest point: Jabal Hafib 1,189 m (3,901 ft)

Population (2006 est.) 2,602,713

Form of government multiparty republic with one appointed council

Armed forces army 44,000; navy 2,500; air force 4,800

Largest cities Dubai (1,225,137); Abu Dhabi (capital – 633,136); Sharjah (584,286)

Official language Arabic

Ethnic composition Emirati 19%; other Arab and Iranian 23%; South Asian 50%; others 8%

Official religion Islam

Religious affiliations Sunni Muslim 80%; Shi'ite Muslim 16%; Christian 3.8%; others 0.2%

Currency 1 Emirati dirham (AED) = 100 fils

Gross domestic product (2006) U.S. $129.4 billion

Gross domestic product per capita (2006) U.S. $49,700

Life expectancy at birth male 72.92 yr; female 78.08 yr

Major resources petroleum, natural gas, camels, cattle, fish, fruit, vegetables, goats, sheep, tourism

QATAR

The Emirate of Qatar occupies the peninsula of the same name. The land is mainly flat, apart from hills in the west and some cliffs in the northeast. Vegetation is most abundant in the north, and wildlife is mainly desert-dwelling creatures. Modern farming methods enable fruit and vegetables to be grown, but most food is imported. The country's wealth is based on its limited oil reserves, but this is increasingly supplemented by exploitation of natural gas—of which the emirate has the world's third largest reserves. Other industries include steel, cement, petrochemicals, and fertilizers. Qatar has one of the world's fastest-growing economies.

NATIONAL DATA – QATAR

Land area 11,437 sq km (4,416 sq mi)

Climate	Altitude m (ft)	Temperatures January °C(°F)	Annual July °C(°F)	precipitation mm (in)
Doha	11 (36)	17 (63)	35 (94)	81 (3.2)

Population (2006 est.) 885,359

Form of government absolute monarchy

Armed forces army 8,500; navy 1,800; air force 2,100

Capital city Doha (358,098)

Official language Arabic

Ethnic composition Arab 40%; Indian 18%; Pakistani 18%; Iranian 10%; other 14%

Official religion Islam

Religious affiliations Muslim 92.4%; Christian 5.9%; Hindu 1.1%; others 0.6%

Currency 1 Qatari rial (QAR) = 100 dirhams

Gross domestic product (2006) U.S. $26.05 billion

Gross domestic product per capita (2006) U.S. $29,400

Life expectancy at birth male 71.37 yr; female 76.57 yr

Major resources petroleum, natural gas, fish, steel and cement, petrochemicals, fertilizer, fodder, fruit, livestock, vegetables

BAHRAIN

Bahrain consists of about 30 islands in the Gulf of Bahrain, in the Persian Gulf. Several of the islands are linked by causeways, and the huge King Fahd causeway links the main island of Bahrain to Saudi Arabia, with which Bahrain has close relations. Bahrain's prosperity is based mainly on natural gas and oil, but reserves are dwindling. Aluminum processing has grown in importance, and Bahrain is also a major banking and communication center. It has a big immigrant workforce.

NATIONAL DATA – BAHRAIN

Land area 665 sq km (257 sq mi)

Climate	Altitude m (ft)	Temperatures January °C(°F)	July °C(°F)	Annual precipitation mm (in)
Al Manamah	6 (18)	17 (63)	34 (93)	70 (2.7)

Major physical features largest island: Bahrain 583 sq km (225 sq mi); highest point: Durkan Hill 134 m (440 ft)

Population (2006 est.) 698,585

Form of government constitutional hereditary monarchy with one appointed council

Armed forces army 8,500; navy 1,200; air force 1,500

Capital city Al Manamah (148,622)

Official language Arabic

Ethnic composition Bahraini 62.4%; non-Bahraini 37.6%

Official religion Islam

Religious affiliations Muslim (Shi'a and Sunni) 81.2%; Christian 9%; other 9.8%

Currency 1 Bahraini dinar (BHD) = 1,000 fils

Gross domestic product (2006) U.S. $17.7 billion

Gross domestic product per capita (2006) U.S. $25,300

Life expectancy at birth male 71.97 yr; female 77 yr

Major resources oil, natural gas, aluminum processing, fisheries, pearls, dates, eggs, livestock, lucerne, vegetables

KUWAIT

Kuwait consists largely of undulating sandy plains, and most of the country is barren desert. The shortage of water in the country means that three-quarters of supplies must be distilled from seawater or imported. In 1990 Kuwait was occupied by Iraq, regaining its sovereignty only after a war in which both countries sustained much economic and environmental damage. Intensive farming enables crops such as melons to be grown. Pollution has damaged the fishing industry. Oil accounts for most of the export revenue, with chemical fertilizers and natural gas supplies making up the rest.

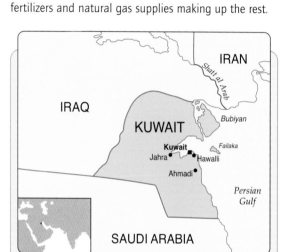

NATIONAL DATA – KUWAIT

Land area 17,820 sq km (6,880 sq mi)

Climate	Altitude m (ft)	Temperatures January °C(°F)	July °C(°F)	Annual precipitation mm (in)
Kuwait City	5 (16)	13 (55)	37 (98)	99 (3.9)

Major physical features highest point: ash-Shaqaya 290 m (951 ft)

Population (2006 est.) 2,418,393

Form of government nonparty constitutional monarchy with one legislative house

Armed forces army 11,000; navy 2,000; air force 2,500

Capital city Kuwait City (67,103)

Official language Arabic

Ethnic composition Kuwaiti 45%; other Arab 35%; South Asian 9%; Iranian 4%; other 7%

Religious affiliations Muslim 85% (Sunni 70%; Shi'a 30%); Christian, Hindu, Parsi, and other 15%

Currency 1 Kuwaiti dinar (KD) = 1,000 fils

Gross domestic product (2006) U.S. $52.17 billion

Gross domestic product per capita (2006) U.S. $21,600

Life expectancy at birth male 76.13 yr; female 78.31 yr

Major resources petroleum, fisheries, shrimps, natural gas, chemical fertilizers, dates, fruits, goats, sheep, vegetables

TURKMENISTAN

The landscape of Turkmenistan consists mainly of the featureless, bleak plains of the Kara Kum Desert. Near the Iranian border the earthquake-prone mountains of the Kopet Dag are flanked by oases—the most popular area for settlement. The climate is generally arid, with hot summers and cold winters. The country joined the Commonwealth of Independent States after the breakup of the Soviet Union, and is now ruled by the autocratic President Niyazov (b. 1940). Cotton, oil, and gas have been the mainstays of the country's economy, but bad debts reduced revenues in the late 1990s. Nevertheless, Turkmenistan has rich mineral resources and thus the potential for growth.

NATIONAL DATA – TURKMENISTAN

Land area 488,100 sq km (188,456 sq mi)

Climate Continental

Major physical features highest point: Mount Ayrybaba 3,137 m (10,292 ft); longest river: Amu Darya (part) 2,539 km (1,578 mi)

Population (2006 est.) 5,042,920

Form of government multiparty republic with two legislative houses

Armed forces army 21,000; navy 700; air force 4,300

Largest cities Ashgabat (capital - 848,444); Türkmenabat (240,880)

Official language Turkmenian

Ethnic composition Turkmen 85%; Uzbek 5%; Russian 4%; other 6%

Religious affiliations Muslim 89%; Eastern Orthodox 9%; unknown 2%

Currency 1 Turkmen manat (TMM) = 100 tenge

Gross domestic product (2006) U.S. $45.11 billion

Gross domestic product per capita (2006) U.S. $8,900

Life expectancy at birth male 58.43 yr; female 65.41 yr

Major resources petroleum, natural gas, sulfur, salt, alfalfa, clay, cotton, grapes, gypsum, limestone, melons, sheep, wheat

UZBEKISTAN

The former Soviet republic of Uzbekistan lies amid the deserts of south-central Asia. It was once crossed by the fabled silk road to China. In the extreme eastern region, beyond the capital Tashkent and the Chatkal Mountains, is the fertile Fergana Basin. The climate is mostly semiarid, with cold winters and hot summers. Intensive irrigation has made Uzbekistan a leading cotton producer, but it has partly drained the Aral Sea, devastating local fishing communities. The country is rich in mineral resources, and major manufacturing industries include machinery, textiles, and chemicals.

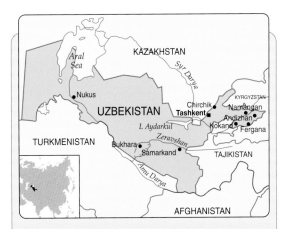

NATIONAL DATA – UZBEKISTAN

Land area 425,400 sq km (164,248 sq mi)

Climate	Altitude m (ft)	Temperatures January °C(°F)	July °C(°F)	Annual precipitation mm (in)
Tashkent	478 (1,569)	1 (34)	25 (77)	417 (16.4)

Major physical features highest point: Beshtor Peak 4,299 m (14,104 ft); largest lake: Aral Sea (part) 66,500 sq km (25,700 sq mi)

Population (2006 est.) 27,307,134

Form of government multiparty republic with one legislative house but under authoritarian presidential rule, with little power outside the executive branch

Armed forces army 40,000; air force 15,000

Largest cities Tashkent (capital - 1,959,190); Namangan (446,237); Andijon (321,622); Samarqand (312,863); Bukhara (249,037); Nukus (240,734)

Official language Uzbek

Ethnic composition Uzbek 80%; Russian 5.5%; Tajik 5%; Kazakh 3%; Karakalpak 2.5%; Tatar 1.5%; other 2.5%

Religious affiliations Muslim 88% (mainly Sunnis); Eastern Orthodox 9%; other 3%

Currency 1 Uzbekistani soum (UZS) = 100 tiyn

Gross domestic product (2006) U.S. $54.81 billion

Gross domestic product per capita (2006) U.S. $2,000

Life expectancy at birth male 61.19 yr; female 68.14 yr

Major resources natural gas, petroleum, coal, gold, uranium, silver, copper, lead and zinc, tungsten, molybdenum, cotton, livestock, fruit, grapes, iron ore, maize/corn, melons, rice, silkworms, sulfur, vegetables, wheat

TAJIKISTAN

Tajikistan lies in the highlands of south-central Asia. Most of eastern Tajikistan is over 3,000 m (10,000 ft) above sea level. In the north lies the fertile Fergana Basin, famed for growing exotic fruits. Tajikistan gained independence in 1991 following the breakup of the Soviet Union, after which there was civil war (1992–97). The country is one of the poorest of the former Soviet republics. Cotton is the main crop, and textiles, carpets, and machinery are among the chief industries.

NATIONAL DATA – TAJIKISTAN

Land area	142,700sq km (55,097 sq mi)			
Climate		Temperatures		Annual
	Altitude m (ft)	January °C(°F)	July °C(°F)	precipitation mm (in)
Dushanbe	796 (2,611)	3 (37)	27 (81)	653 (25.7)

Major physical features highest point: Communism 7,495 m (24,590 ft); longest rivers: Amu Darya (part) 2,539 km (1,578 mi); Vakhsh 800 km (497 mi)

Population (2006 est.) 7,320,815

Form of government multiparty republic with one legislative house

Armed forces army 7,600

Largest cities Dushanbe (capital - 533,495); Khudzhand = Khujand (142,513)

Official language Tajik

Ethnic composition Tajik 79.9%; Uzbek 15.3%; Russian 1.1%; Kyrgyz 1.1%; other 2.6%

Religious affiliations Sunni Muslim 85%; Shi'a Muslim 5%; other 10%

Currency 1 Tajikistan Somoni (TJ or TJK) = 100 dirams

Gross domestic product (2006) U.S. $9.405 billion

Gross domestic product per capita (2006) U.S. $1,300

Life expectancy at birth male 62.03 yr; female 68 yr

Major resources hydropower, some petroleum, uranium, mercury, brown coal, lead, zinc, tungsten, silver, gold, cotton, wool, cattle, antimony, apricots, fruits, livestock, niobium, phosphates, rice, silkworms, tantalum, vanadium

KYRGYZSTAN

The mountainous republic of Kyrgyzstan lies in central Asia. The massive Tien Shan mountain range dominates the country, extending along the border with China. Elsewhere other ranges are cut by deep river valleys and basins. The mountains bring plentiful water to an otherwise desert region. In 1991, after the breakup of the Soviet Union, Kyrgyzstan joined the Commonwealth of Independent States. The main agricultural activity is livestock rearing, and grain, cotton, and tobacco are also grown. Plentiful resources and hydroelectric power have benefited industries such as textiles, food processing, and weaving.

NATIONAL DATA – KYRGYZSTAN

Land area	191,300 sq km (73,861 sq mi)			
Climate		Temperatures		Annual
	Altitude m (ft)	January °C(°F)	July °C(°F)	precipitation mm (in)
Bishkek	828 (2,716)	-3 (27)	25 (77)	442 (17.4)

Major physical features highest point: Pobeda Peak 7,439 m (24,406 ft); longest river: Syr Darya (part) 2,204 km (1,370 mi)

Population (2006 est.) 5,213,898

Form of government multiparty republic with two legislative houses

Armed forces army 8,500; air force 4,000

Capital city Bishkek (933,763)

Official languages Kyrghyz, Russian

Ethnic composition Kyrgyz 64.9%; Uzbek 13.8%; Russian 12.5%; Dungan 1.1%; Ukrainian 1%; Uygur 1%; other 5.7%

Religious affiliations Muslim 75%; Russian Orthodox 20%; other 5%

Currency 1 Kyrgyzstani Som (KGS) = 100 tyiyn

Gross domestic product (2006) U.S. $10.49 billion

Gross domestic product per capita (2006) U.S. $2,000

Life expectancy at birth male 64.48 yr; female 72.7 yr

Major resources hydropower, gold, uranium, coal, oil, natural gas, nepheline, mercury, bismuth, lead, zinc, antimony, cotton, fruit, vegetables, grapes, livestock, sugar beet, tobacco

KAZAKHSTAN

Kazakhstan is the second largest of the former Soviet republics, after Russia. The mainly flat landscape is broken by mountain ranges in the southeast and east, and more than two-thirds of the country is desert or semidesert, with salty lakes and marshes. The climate is characterized by intense winter cold and summer heat. Kazakhstan gained independence in 1991, but tensions between Kazakhs and ethnic Russians remain. The country is rich in minerals, with huge oil reserves. Agriculture employs about one-quarter of the people.

NATIONAL DATA – KAZAKHSTAN

Land area   2,669,800 sq km (1,030,816 sq mi)

Climate		Temperatures		Annual
	Altitude m (ft)	January °C(°F)	July °C(°F)	precipitation mm (in)
Almaty	775 (2,543)	-6 (21)	24 (75)	641 (25.2)

Major physical features   highest point: Khan-Tengri 7,199 m (23,620 ft); lowest point: Mangyshlak Depression -132 m (-433 ft); longest river: Irtysh (part) 4,400 km (2,760 mi)

Population   (2006 est.) 15,233,244

Form of government   multiparty republic with two legislative houses but with authoritarian presidential rule

Armed forces   army 46,800; air force 19,000

Largest cities   Almaty (1,227,059); Chimkent (420,435); Karaganda (404,451); Taraz (366,761); Astana (capital – 356,886); Pavlodar (330,165)

Official language   Kazakh

Ethnic composition   Kazakh (Qazaq) 53.4%; Russian 30%; Ukrainian 3.7%; Uzbek 2.5%; German 2.4%; Tatar 1.7%; Uygur 1.4%; other 4.9%

Religious affiliations   Muslim 47%; Russian Orthodox 44%; other 9%

Currency   1 tenge (KZT) = 100 tiyin

Gross domestic product   (2006) U.S. $138.7 billion

Gross domestic product per capita   (2006) U.S. $9,100

Life expectancy at birth   male 61.56 yr; female 72.52 yr

Major resources   coal, oil, natural gas, iron ore, bauxite, copper, nickel, lead, gold, uranium, cereals, cotton

MONGOLIA

Most of huge, lofty, landlocked Mongolia is dry steppe grassland, and the rest is mainly cold, arid wasteland. Most of the south of the country is occupied by the stony Gobi Desert. Much of the country is prone to earthquakes. Huge numbers of livestock are grazed on Mongolia's grasslands, including sheep, cattle, goats, and horses. Crop farming is minimal. Most industries are based on processing raw materials, and the principal export products are minerals and animal products.

NATIONAL DATA – MONGOLIA

Land area   1,564,116 sq km (603,909 sq mi)

Climate		Temperatures		Annual
	Altitude m (ft)	January °C(°F)	July °C(°F)	precipitation mm (in)
Ulaanbaatar	1,337 (4,385)	-20 (4)	18 (64)	271 (10.6)

Major physical features   highest point: Hüyten (Nayramdal) Peak 4,374 m (14,350 ft); longest river: Selenga 998 km (620 mi)

Population   (2006 est.) 2,832,224

Form of government   mixed parliamentary/presidential multiparty republic with one legislative house

Armed forces   army 7,500; air force 800

Capital city   Ulaanbaatar (881,218)

Official language   Khalkha Mongolian

Ethnic composition   Mongol (mainly Khalkha) 94.9%; Turkic (mainly Kazakh) 5%; other (including Chinese and Russian) 0.1%

Religious affiliations   Buddhist Lamaist 50%; none 40%; Shamanist and Christian 6%; Muslim 4%

Currency   1 tögrög/tugrik (MNT) = 100 mongos

Gross domestic product   (2006) U.S. $5.781 billion

Gross domestic product per capita   (2006) U.S. $2,000

Life expectancy at birth   male 62.64 yr; female 67.25 yr

Major resources   oil, coal, copper, molybdenum, tungsten, phosphates, tin, nickel, zinc, fluorspar, gold, silver, iron, livestock, cereals, hay fodder, lignite, potatoes, vegetables, wolfram

CHINA

NATIONAL DATA – CHINA

Land area 9,326,410 sq km (3,600,947 sq mi)

Climate	Altitude m (ft)	Temperatures January °C(°F)	July °C(°F)	Annual precipitation mm (in)
Hami (near Urumqi)	738 (2,421)	–11 (12)	27 (81)	35 (1.4)
Guangzhou	63 (201)	14 (56)	28 (83)	1,678 (66.1)
Beijing	51 (167)	–5 (23)	26 (79)	635 (25)
Harbin	172 (564)	–19 (–3)	23 (73)	521 (20.5)

Major physical features highest point: Mount Everest 8,850 m (29,035 ft); lowest point: Turfan depression -154 m (-505 ft); longest river: Yangtze (Chang) 5,525 km (3,434 mi)

Population (2006 est.) 1,313,973,713

Form of government communist state

Armed forces army 1,600,000; navy 255,000; air force 400,000

Largest cities Shanghai (15,434,642); Beijing (capital - 7,724,932); Hong Kong (6,940,432); Wuhan (4,287,693); Chengdu (3,972,509); Tianjin (3,755,249); Shenyang (3,564,751)

Official language Standard Mandarin

Ethnic composition Han Chinese 91.9%; Chuang 1.4%; Manchu 0.9%; Hui 0.8%; Miao 0.7%; Uighur 0.6%; Yi 0.6%; Tuchia 0.5%; Mongolian 0.4%; Tibetan 0.4%; others 1.7%

Religious affiliations Nonreligious 71.2%; Chinese folk religion 20.1%; Buddhist 6.0%; Muslim 2.4%; Christian 0.2%; others 0.1%

Currency 1 yuan (CNY) or Renminbi (RMB) = 10 jiao = 10 fen

Gross domestic product (2006) U.S. $10 trillion

Gross domestic product per capita (2006) U.S. $7,600

Life expectancy at birth male 70.89 yr; female 74.46 yr

Major resources coal, iron ore, petroleum, natural gas, mercury, tin, tungsten, antimony, manganese, molybdenum, vanadium, magnetite, aluminum, lead, zinc, uranium, hydropower, fisheries, tourism, asbestos, copper, cotton, jute and hemp, livestock, mercury, phosphate rock, rice, salt, soybeans, sugar beet, sulfur, tea, timber, tobacco, wheat

Occupying nearly one-quarter of the Asian landmass and bordering 14 other nations, China is the world's third largest country. It is also the most populous and has a civilization that dates back thousands of years. China has been the cradle of some of the most important scientific and technical discoveries ever made, as well as a place of great cultural influence.

Geography

In southwestern China the Tibetan Plateau, at 4,500 m (15,000 ft), is the highest in the world. On its southern edge are the great Himalayas, and on its eastern side the sources of the Mekong, Yangtze, and Huang Rivers. North and northeast of the plateau lie the desert wastes of Xinjiang and Inner Mongolia. Farther northeast is the edge of the Gobi Desert, and beyond is the fertile Manchurian Plain. Southeast of Manchuria the north China plains surround a vast inlet of the Yellow Sea. The capital, Beijing, is located on this highly populated lowland. China's southern coast is irregular

and often steep; the southeast coast is tropical. Climate varies widely over such a vast region, from hot summer monsoons and cyclones in the southeast to bitterly cold winters in the west and north. Extensive forests remain in places, ranging from evergreen broadleaf to tropical rain forest. Steppe turns to scrub before petering out in the desert basins of the northwest. Animal life is varied and includes yaks, red pandas, giant pandas (found only in the bamboo forests of Sichuan), camels, leopards, tigers, civets, gazelles, buffalo, and monkeys.

Society

For 3,000 years from about 1700 B.C.E. China was an empire. During that time the Chinese were the first to invent gunpowder, paper, printing, silk, and porcelain, as well as various forms of medicine. They built elaborate palaces and other buildings, and explored distant lands.

The Great Wall, begun in about 300 B.C., was built to keep northern invaders out. It is over 6,000 km (3,728 m) long in total.

MAO ZEDONG'S FAILED INITIATIVES

After the defeat of the nationalists in 1949 the People's Republic of China was proclaimed under Mao Zedong. His plan was to improve the failing economy by using production methods modeled on those of the Soviet Union and with Soviet loans. In 1958 he launched the "Great Leap Forward," utilizing the rural workforce on a massive scale, but it proved a disastrous failure and led to Soviet aid being halted. In 1966 another initiative, the "Great Proletarian Cultural Revolution" led only to anarchy and violence. His death led to a period of more moderate government.

The fall of the last Chinese emperor in 1912 marked the start of social and political upheaval that culminated in the establishment of a communist republic in 1949. Under the rule of Mao Zedong (1893-1976) life was often harsh. Later rulers have reduced China's world isolation but have often been illiberal as well.

Economy

Since the 1970s China has moved away from a Soviet-style command economy. The economy is still centrally planned, but not all businesses are owned by the state. Since the 1980s ventures with other countries, as well as foreign loans, have been encouraged. China's economy has an extremely high growth rate, although the regions have not benefited equally from the boom.

Only about one-tenth of the land is suitable for cultivation, and rice is the main crop. Livestock grazing is important. Fish—from the surrounding seas and freshwater fisheries—is important in the Chinese diet. China has huge mineral wealth and is the world's largest producer and consumer of coal. Energy comes from coal, hydroelectricity, and nuclear power. Heavy industry has given way to industries such as the production of fertilizers, textiles, and electronics. China's primary trading partners are Japan and the United States.

Railroads connect every province and region, but many roads outside cities are unsurfaced. Waterways carry more than one-third of internal freight. China has a large merchant fleet and many international airports.

TAIWAN

Formerly Formosa, the independent state of Taiwan claims to be the sole legitimate Republic of China (its official name)—a reflection of the fact that in 1949 it was the last refuge for China's nationalist government after defeat by the communists on the mainland. Taiwan also has jurisdiction over 80 or so small islands.

Geography

Despite the fact that Taiwan is only 160 km (100 mi) from the Chinese mainland, its landscape is different; the high mountainous interior with its lush vegetation is

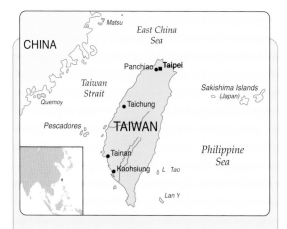

NATIONAL DATA – TAIWAN

Land area	32,260 sq km (12,460 sq mi)			
Climate		Temperatures		Annual
	Altitude m (ft)	January °C(°F)	July °C(°F)	precipitation mm (in)
Taipei	9 (30)	16 (61)	29 (84)	2,129 (83.8)

Major physical features highest point: Yü Shan 3,997 m (13,113 ft)

Population (2006 est.) 23,036,087

Form of government multiparty republic with two legislative houses

Armed forces army 200,000; navy 45,000; air force 45,000

Largest cities Taipei (capital – 2,468,705); Kaohsiung (1,519,748); Taichung (1,124,514); Tainan (737,271)

Official language Mandarin Chinese

Ethnic composition Taiwanese 84%; mainland Chinese 14%; Aboriginal 2%

Religious affiliations Chinese folk religion 48.5%; Buddhist 43%; Christian 7.4%; Muslim 0.5%; others 0.6%

Currency 1 New Taiwan Dollar (NTD) = 100 cents

Gross domestic product (2006) U.S. $668.3 billion

Gross domestic product per capita (2006) U.S. $29,000

Life expectancy at birth male 74.67 yr; female 80.47 yr

Major resources coal, natural gas, dolomite/limestone, marble, asbestos, salt, fisheries, rice, bananas, citrus fruits, pigs, pineapples, poultry, sulfur, sugarcane, sweet potatoes, timber

fringed with flat coastal plains, sandy beaches, and forests. The mountains of the Central Range rise steeply from the eastern coast. On the range's western side the land drops gently to a coastline fringed with dunes and lagoons. Near the capital, Taipei, there is an area of volcanic activity. Yangmingshan National Park is noted for its volcanic peaks, sulfurous craters, lakes, and rivers. The country has a subtropical monsoon climate, with typhoons likely to strike several times a year. Over half the island is covered in forest, ranging from laurels and acacias to conifers and tropical evergreens, bamboos, and palms, depending on altitude. Animals include the Asian black bear, foxes, deer, and various monkey species; the Taiwan macaque is unique to the island. Bird life is plentiful, including 220 native species.

Taiwan's outstanding natural beauty, with forested mountainsides, is exemplified by this view of Tienhsaing, in Taroko National Park.

Society

The Chinese knew about Taiwan in the 7th century A.D., but did not settle there. The first European settlers (Dutch traders) were driven out in 1661 by Zheng Cheng-gong (1624–62), and the Qing regime captured the island in 1683. Soon a flood of immigrants arrived from the mainland, establishing the island's economic importance. Japan held the island until defeat in World War II, when nationalist China took control. In 1949 Chinese communists routed the nationalists on the mainland, forcing them to flee to Taiwan, where they set up a government, still claiming to be the legitimate rulers of China. The United States. provided economic and military aid, preventing communist attacks on the island. In 1991 Taiwan formally ended its 30-year state of war with the People's Republic.

Economy

Cheap, plentiful labor and vigorous marketing of Taiwanese products has fueled dramatic growth of the economy since the 1950s, making the island one of the most powerful economies in Asia. Farming was the lifeblood of the economy, but today some food is imported to meet demand. Rice is the main crop. Half the island supports forest, but timber quality is poor, and many areas are inaccessible to loggers. Fish, especially tuna, are plentiful in the surrounding waters.

Minerals are limited; marble and dolomite are quarried, and salt is produced in coastal pans. Both hydroelectric and nuclear power have been developed. Manufacturing is the mainstay of the economy. Electrical and electronic goods, textiles, and garments are key exports. Taiwan is also a world leader in the production of computer hardware and semiconductors.

Roads are well developed but often crowded. The main railroad encircles the island. There are ports capable of berthing large ships, and good internal and international air links. Taiwan has a well-developed healthcare program, and there is adequate housing for most people. Schooling is free and compulsory from six to 18, with opportunities for higher education.

THE TAIWANESE PEOPLE

Taiwan has long been a refuge for those fleeing the Chinese mainland, and at other times it has been dominated by European and Japanese colonists. Today, however, the island is discovering its own identity. Taiwan is one of the world's most densely populated countries. Most of the people are ethnic Taiwanese, descended from 17th-century Chinese settlers. A large minority—called mainlanders—is made up of postwar refugees and their descendants, who speak Mandarin Chinese, now the official language. The principal religions are Buddhism, Taoism, and Confucianism.

The communist republic of North Korea occupies the northern half of the Korean Peninsula. North Korea consists of rugged uplands and mountains, with its highest peak, Mount Paektu, on the border with China. The two largest rivers, the Yalu and the Tumen, rise here and form the northern border. The only extensive lowland areas are on the western side of the country. Winters are cold and frosty, and summers are warm and humid. Coniferous trees clad the mountains, where tigers, leopards, and many bird species can be found.

NATIONAL DATA – KOREA, NORTH

Land area	120,410 sq km (46,490 sq mi)			

Climate	Altitude m (ft)	Temperatures January °C(°F)	July °C(°F)	Annual precipitation mm (in)
P'yongyang	27 (89)	-8 (18)	25 (77)	824 (32.4)

Major physical features highest point: Mount Paektu 2,750 m (9,002 ft); longest river: Yalu 806 km (501 mi)

Population (2006 est.) 23,113,019

Form of government one-party communist republic with one legislative house

Armed forces army 950,000; navy 46,000; air force 110,000

Largest cities P'yongyang (capital – 3,059,678); Hamhung (569,994); Namp'o (458,903)

Official language Korean

Ethnic composition Korean 99.8%; Chinese 0.2%

Religious affiliations Nonreligious 67.9%; traditional beliefs 15.6%; Ch'ondogyo 13.9%; Buddhist 1.7%; Christian 0.9%

Currency 1 North Korean won (KPW) = 100 chon

Gross domestic product (2006) U.S. $40 billion

Gross domestic product per capita (2006) U.S. $1,800

Life expectancy at birth male 68.92 yr; female 74.51 yr

Major resources coal, lead, tungsten, zinc, graphite, magnesite, iron ore, copper, gold, pyrites, salt, fluorspar, hydropower, barley, beans, cattle, fisheries, grain, pigs, poultry, rice, tobacco, timber, wheat

This elaborate palace facade, with gold statues in the foreground, belies North Korea's chronic problems. A failed communist-style regime continues to bring poverty and hardship to the people.

North Korea has been under communist rule since 1948. In 1950 North Korea invaded South Korea in an attempt at reunification, but was thwarted by the United States. More recently, North Korea's weapons (including nuclear) programs cause concern to the international community. Attempts at transforming the agricultural economy into a self-sufficient industrialized one have been only partially successful. The country was critically dependent on food aid in the 1990s, and many people died of starvation—owing partly to poor farming methods. Rice is the main crop, although the fishing industry has expanded. Iron ore is the chief mineral resource, and iron and related products are major exports. Money sent home from North Koreans working in Russia and Japan is the main foreign currency earner.

KOREA, SOUTH

South Korea occupies the southern half of the Korean Peninsula. The terrain is rugged and often mountainous, with the population crowded into the few lowland areas. Running from north to south, parallel with the east coast, are the Taebaek Mountains; they contain the source of several rivers, such as the Han and the Naktong. The densely populated Han Basin includes the capital, Seoul. The western and southern coasts are riddled with channels and islands. Cold North Asian winds blow in winter, but in summer warm, humid Pacific air blows in. Fall may see the risk of typhoons. About two-thirds of South Korea is forested. Boars and deer remain, but bears, tigers, and leopards are rare.

South Korea was founded in 1948. Since then it has experienced numerous constitutions and periods of military rule. The country was invaded by North Korea in 1950 in an attempt to reunite the peninsula by force, but the bid failed. Despite government backing for heavy industry, economic success has been limited. Farming is practiced in the lowland areas, and most farms are family owned. Rice is the staple crop, and silk and tobacco are exported. South Korea has few mineral resources but exports some iron ore and tungsten. Manufacturing is the backbone of the economy and industry. Chemicals, metals, machinery, and electronics are especially important. The country is a major producer of silicon chips.

Much of South Korea is mountainous, and the majority of the population lives in cities located in the lowlands.

NATIONAL DATA – KOREA, SOUTH

Land area 98,190 sq km (37,911 sq mi)

Climate	Altitude m (ft)	Temperatures January °C(°F)	July °C(°F)	Annual precipitation mm (in)
Seoul	295 (968)	-5 (23)	25 (77)	1,250 (49.2)

Major physical features highest point: Halla San (Cheju island) 1,950 m (6,398 ft); longest river: Han 470 km (292 mi)

Population (2006 est.) 48,846,823

Form of government multiparty republic with one legislative house

Armed forces army 560,000; navy 63,000; air force 64,000

Largest cities Seoul (capital – 10,451,281); Pusan (3,663,421); Inch'on (2,657,698); Taegu (2,591,996); Taejon (1,515,270)

Official language Korean

Ethnic composition Korean 99.9%; Chinese 0.1%

Religious affiliations no affiliation 46%; Christian 26%; Buddhist 26%; Confucianist 1%; other 1%

Currency 1 South Korean won (KRW) = 100 chon

Gross domestic product (2006) U.S. $1.18 trillion

Gross domestic product per capita (2006) U.S. $24,200

Life expectancy at birth male 73.61 yr; female 80.75 yr

Major resources coal, tungsten, graphite, molybdenum, lead, hydropower, barley, beans, fish, fruits, vegetables, gold, iron ore, lignite, maize/corn, millet, potatoes, rice, sorghum, sugar, timber, tobacco, wheat

JAPAN

NATIONAL DATA – JAPAN

Land area 374,744 sq km (144,689 sq mi)

Climate		Temperatures		Annual
	Altitude m (ft)	January °C(°F)	July °C(°F)	precipitation mm (in)
Sapporo	18 (59)	-4 (74)	21 (90)	1,128 (44.4)
Tokyo	6 (20)	6 (43)	26 (79)	1,467 (57.7)

Major physical features highest point: Mount Fuji 3,776 m (12,388 ft); largest lake: Biwa 673 sq km (260 sq mi)

Population (2006 est.) 127,463,611

Form of government multiparty constitutional monarchy with two legislative houses

Armed forces army 45,600; marine self-defense force 44,000; naval aviation 9,800; ground self-defense force 148,200

Largest cities Tokyo (capital – 8,403,512); Yokohama (3,632,023); Osaka (2,588,578); Nagoya (2,197,711); Sapporo (1,908,433); Kobe (1,541,229)

Official language Japanese

Ethnic composition Japanese 99%; others 1% (Korean, Chinese, Brazilian, Filipino, other)

Religious affiliations Shinto and Buddhist 84%; Christian 0.7%; other 15.3%

Currency 1 yen (JPY) = 100 sen

Gross domestic product (2006) U.S. $4.911 trillion

Gross domestic product per capita (2006) U.S. $33,100

Life expectancy at birth male 77.96 yr; female 84.7 yr

Major resources coal, edible seaweeds, fisheries, fruit, potatoes, poultry, rice, shellfish, silk, sulfur, sweet potatoes, tea, timber, vegetables

Japan is an archipelago of about 4,000 islands lying across a fault line off the east coast of Asia. The country isolated itself from other cultures for 200 years until the mid-19th century, helping create a uniform, feudal society. However, Japan has since transformed itself into a dynamic, wealthy 21st-century industrial nation.

Geography

Japan's islands form a 2,500-km- (1,500-mi-) long arc. The country is prone to earthquakes, volcanoes, tidal waves, and hurricanes. Mountains and thick forest cover two-thirds of the land area and have effectively confined settlement, agriculture, and industry to the coastal plains. Honshu is the largest and most populous of the four main islands; the other three being (from north to south) Hokkaido, Shikoku, and Kyushu. At the heart of Honshu are the Japanese Alps, and southeast of here lies volcanic Mount Fuji. Honshu also contains Japan's biggest lowland area, with Tokyo, the capital, on its southern side. Japan has a monsoon-type climate.

Sacred Mount Fuji, Japan's highest peak, rises majestically from a flat plain to tower over Tagonoura port on Honshu.

Winters are cold and summers are hot and humid. Destructive typhoons occur in late summer. Bamboo forests are found as far north as Tokyo and provide timber. Cherry trees are found everywhere. Other vegetation zones include semitropical rain forest, Japanese cedars, broadleaf forests, conifers, and alpine shrubs. Japan's wildlife includes boars, bears, monkeys, lizards, snakes, and the 1.5-m- (5-ft-) long Japanese giant salamander. Insect and birdlife are also abundant.

Society

Until the 19th century, Japan operated as a closed feudal society and was virtually unknown to foreigners. Following the enforced end to isolationism in 1853, the Japanese embarked on rapid social and economic change, freely adapting to Western technologies. Since defeat in World War II Japanese society has achieved overwhelming industrial success within one generation. Most Japanese are Mongoloid in origin, although the Ainu people of Hokkaido are survivors of an older Caucasian people that once lived all over Japan.

Economy

Japan's marketing tactics and competitive prices have won it an ever-increasing share of world markets. Agriculture employs only a small proportion of the workforce, and food exports account for only a tiny percentage of income. Most of the larger farms are on Hokkaido. Rice is the main crop, grown over most of the country. Livestock and vegetables are also farmed, and Japan has a large fishing fleet. It also argues for a resumption of whaling.

Japan has few minerals, and most raw materials are imported. Over one-third of the workforce is employed in manufacturing or construction, which provide about two-fifths of GDP. Products include high-quality items such as electrical and electronic goods, processed foods, motor vehicles, and chemicals. Japan is also a major shipbuilding nation. Other key products include synthetic fibers, paper, cement, iron, and steel.

Japan has well-developed road and railroad links within and between the islands. The country is also a principal seagoing nation, with ports serving all of the main urban areas. Air transportation is also well developed. Postal and telecommunications are among the best in the world. Social infrastructure is also good.

JAPANESE CULTURE AND TRADITION

The Japanese have a highly developed, long-standing and refined cultural tradition. It can range from the codes of honor that guided the lives of the samurai, or warrior classes, of the old feudal system to the elaborate rituals of the tea ceremony. In recent years, however, some Western ideas have been adopted. Conversely, many Japanese traditions have found a worldwide appeal, notably in recreation and sport. For example, judo and karate are popular in many countries outside Japan. Japanese cinema, too, has achieved international recognition as an art form.

IRAN

A mountainous country in southwestern Asia, Iran is one of the largest of the Gulf states and shares borders with 10 other countries. The Iranian plateau was the home of the ancient Persian civilizations, and its cultural heritage goes back 5,000 years.

NATIONAL DATA –IRAN

Land area	1,636,000 sq km (631,663 sq mi)			

Climate	Altitude m (ft)	Temperatures January °C(°F)	July °C(°F)	Annual precipitation mm (in)
Tehran	1,220 (4,002)	3 (37)	30 (86)	230 (9)
Abadan	2 (7)	12 (54)	36 (97)	193 (7.5)

Major physical features highest point: Damavand 5,771 m (18,934 ft); longest river: Karun 850 km (528 mi)

Population (2006 est.) 68,688,433

Form of government theocratic republic

Armed forces army 350,000; Islamic revolutionary guard corps 125,000; navy 18,000; air force 52,000

Largest cities Tehran (capital – 7,185,831); Mashhad (2,463,393); Esfahan (1,600,554); Karaj (1,602,350); Tabriz (1,496,319); Shiraz (1,307,552)

Official language Farsi (Persian)

Ethnic composition Persian 51%; Azeri 24%; Gilaki and Mazandarani 8%; Kurd 7%; Arab 3%; Lur 2%; Baloch 2%; Turkmen 2%; other 1%

Official religion Islam

Religious affiliations Shi'a Muslim 89%; Sunni Muslim 9%; Zoroastrian, Jewish, Christian, and Baha'i 2%

Currency 10 Iranian rial (IRR) = toman

Gross domestic product (2006) U.S. $610.4 billion

Gross domestic product per capita (2006) U.S. $8,900

Life expectancy at birth male 68.86 yr; female 71.74 yr

Major resources petroleum, natural gas, coal, chromium, copper, iron ore, lead, manganese, zinc, sulfur, building materials, cement, fisheries, textiles, timber, cereals, sugar beet, fruits, nuts, cotton

Geography

Much of Iran is a massive semiarid plateau ringed by mountains. Earthquakes are common. The only large region of fertile land is in the Karun River Basin in Khuzistan. The basin is bounded in the northeast by the Zagros Mountains, and east of the range is a vast plateau lying at an average of 1,200 m (4,000 ft) above sea level. It is characterized by salt deserts and occasional oases. The southeastern side has coastal mountains, while to the east are the peaks of the Baluchistan and Khorasan Mountains. The Elburz Mountains of the north and northeast include several active volcanoes. North of the Elburz range a narrow lowland fronts the marshy shore of the Caspian Sea, broadening to the east into the Turkoman steppe.

The climate ranges from continental to subtropical. The plains and mountains of the north have rain all year around, but in the west and northwest precipitation falls mainly in winter. Elsewhere it is much drier. Plant life thrives on the shores of the

The pillars of Persepolis, the ancient capital of Persia, are still standing, despite the city being sacked by Alexander the Great in 330 B.C.

Caspian Sea, and the northern slopes of the Elburz Mountains are covered in forests. Elsewhere vegetation is sparse. Iran has a rich variety of animal life and many wildlife sanctuaries. The shoreline of the Caspian Sea is a refuge for numerous waterbirds. However, wildlife in the Persian Gulf suffered badly as a result of oil being released during the Gulf War of 1990–91.

Society

The Iranian plateau has seen the rise and fall of many civilizations, the earliest known being the Elamites, in the 3rd millennium B.C. After World War I Reza Khan (1878-1944) had himself elected shah, changing the country's name from Persia to Iran. He sought to create a modern nation free from foreign domination. He was succeeded by his son Mohammad Reza Shah Pahlavi (1919-80). In 1978 the suppression of antigovernment demonstrations fueled opposition by supporters of exiled religious leader Ayatollah Ruhollah Khomeini (c.1900-89). In 1979 the shah was forced into exile,

Khomeini returned in triumph from exile, and an Islamic republic was formed. The same year Islamic militants seized 66 American hostages from the U.S. embassy and did not release them until 1981. The West, supported by Arab countries fearing the spread of Islamic revolution, applied sanctions. More recently, Iran has been accused of being a sponsor of terrorism through its activities in Lebanon and elsewhere, and there are concerns about its nuclear weapon ambitions. Sanctions remain in place.

Economy

The economy depends almost entirely on petroleum, which for many years brought prosperity. The Islamic revolution, the Iran–Iraq War, and fluctuating oil prices have hampered stable economic progress, however. Good arable land is scarce, and yields are low, and much of the nation's food is imported. But forestry and fisheries are well developed. Main minerals include coal and metal ores, but only oil and gas have been fully exploited, and Iran is self-sufficient in energy needs. Apart from traditional textiles—Persian carpets and rugs—most of the manufacturing sector has been developed since 1954. Products range from processed food to petrochemicals and armaments.

Railroads are designed for long-distance travel on major routes, but local traffic uses poorly maintained roads. Healthcare is free to the poor, but many rural areas lack medical supplies and trained staff. Education is compulsory and free, but illiteracy is widespread.

GOVERNMENT IN IRAN

In 1979 the rule of Islamic fundamentalism was instigated under Ayatollah Ruhollah Khomeini and has continued after his death. Under the 1979 constitution, supreme authority in all matters rests with the Islamic spiritual leader, or *valiy-e faqih*. The president and the 270-member parliament (the Majles) are freely elected for a four-year term. The president appoints the cabinet, which is subject to the approval of the Majles and the *valiy-e faqih*. Legislation is vetted by the 12-member Council of Guardians to ensure it conforms to the Islamic constitution. Broadcasting is strictly controlled.

AFGHANISTAN

The landlocked state of Afghanistan lies in the mountains of south-central Asia. For decades the country has been plagued by civil war. In 2005 Afghanistan's first democratically elected president took office, but the country still faces a difficult future.

Geography

The country lies at the heart of southern Asia's great mountain belt. The Hindu Kush and neighboring ranges cover eastern and central Afghanistan—a rugged and

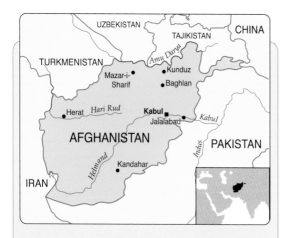

NATIONAL DATA – AFGHANISTAN

Land area	647,500 sq km (250,001 sq mi)			

Climate		Temperatures		Annual
	Altitude m (ft)	January °C(°F)	July °C(°F)	precipitation mm (in)
Kabul	1,815 (5,955)	-1 (30)	24 (76)	311 (12.2)

Major physical features highest point: Mount Nowshak 7,485 m (24,557 ft); longest river: Helmand (part) 1,400 km (870 mi)

Population (2006 est.) 31,056,997

Form of government Islamic republic

Armed forces army 27,000

Largest cities Kabul (capital – 3,199,091); Kandahar (411,727); Mazar-i-Sharif (326,737)

Official languages Pashto, Dari Persian

Ethnic composition Pashtun 42%; Tajik 27%; Hazara 9%; Uzbek 9%; Aimak 4%; Turkmen 3%; Baloch 2%; other 4%

Religious affiliations Sunni Muslim 80%; Shi'a Muslim 19%; other 1%

Currency 1 afghani (AFA) = 1 puls

Gross domestic product (2004) U.S. $21.5 billion

Gross domestic product per capita (2004) U.S. $800

Life expectancy at birth male 43.16 yr; female 43.53 yr

Major resources natural gas, petroleum, coal, copper, chromite, talc, barites, sulfur, lead, zinc, iron ore, salt, precious and semiprecious stones, barley, cotton, fruit, goats, maize/corn, nuts, rice, sheep, sugar beet, vegetables, wheat

inhospitable region prone to earthquakes. The northern plains adjoining the Amu Darya River are fertile and densely populated. South of the mountains the deserts and salt flats of the broader southwestern plateau are sparsely watered by rivers flowing from the Hindu Kush.

The extreme climate of cold winters and hot summers is typical of semiarid steppe country, although local variations exist. The winter months are coldest in the northeastern mountains. The driest area is in the southwest. The eastern valleys are humid. Vegetation is sparse in the semiarid southwest and in some mountain areas. Elsewhere in the mountains are forests with pine, cedar, and fir, while walnut and oak trees grow at lower levels. Many large animals, including tigers, have all but disappeared, although some bears, gazelles, and snow leopards still survive. Birdlife is a little more plentiful.

Society

Afghanistan has long been disputed by foreign powers anxious to control its strategic position atop the land route to India via the Khyber Pass. The present boundaries are relatively recent. During periods of its early history Afghanistan was part of Persian, and then Greek, empires. Then it fell to a succession of other empires—Parthian, Kushan, and Sasanian Persian—before being conquered by Arabs in the 7th century A.D. Other rulers included the Mongols under Genghis Khan (c.1162–1227). In the 1700s the country became independent but continued to be disturbed by rebellions and ambitious foreign nations. In 1880 Afghanistan became a buffer state between British India and Russia.

Following full independence in 1919 Afghanistan formed a special relationship with the Soviet regime that lasted until 1979. Unrest deposed the ruling shah in 1973, and the country was declared a republic. After another coup in 1978 power passed to the Soviet-backed People's Democratic Party (PDPA) of Afghanistan. This regime was violently opposed by Islamic groups, and in 1979 Soviet forces invaded the country to install a new PDPA government. Fighting lasted nine years and, after Soviet withdrawal, a military council was established. It proved as ineffective as other regimes, however, in maintaining peace. Following the defeat of the Taliban in 2001, a UN-brokered deal led to an interim council,

and an international peacekeeping force was sent to facilitate reconstruction. However, Afghanistan has become a theater of conflict between Islamic insurgents, such as the regrouping Taliban, and peacekeepers.

Economy

Afghanistan's economy has been severely disrupted by war, natural disasters, and political instability. It remains one of the poorest in the world and is heavily reliant on aid to help it achieve growth. Agriculture remains the mainstay of the economy. The principal crop is wheat, but rice, barley, fruit, and cotton are also grown. When the Taliban was in power it halted most of the illegal opium trade by destroying the poppy crops, but many of them have been replanted, and illegal opium trading now accounts for half the country's GDP.

Natural gas is the main mineral resource. Most other available power sources have not been exploited. The chief industry is the manufacture of woolen and cotton textiles, and traditional handicrafts and woven carpets are valuable exports.

The country has a damaged infrastructure, insufficient skilled workforce, and political instability. There are no railroads and few navigable rivers, and most transportation is by road. Education, healthcare, and welfare provision are inadequate.

A high valley in Afghanistan. Most of the population lives in such irrigated valleys on the fringes of the mountains—especially in the fertile valley of the Kabul River in the southeast.

THE THREAT OF THE TALIBAN

In 1996 the fundamentalist Taliban militia gained control of parts of the country. It brought a degree of stability following the war waged by Afghan rebels against the Soviet Union, but the regime was characterized by severely repressive Islamic laws. The economy also suffered under the Taliban's rule. In 2001 the Taliban was found to be harboring al-Qaeda terrorist leader Osama bin Laden, who was blamed for the attacks on the United States on September 11, 2001. With U.S. help the Taliban was driven from power by the Northern Alliance later that year, but is emerging again.

PAKISTAN

Pakistan occupies the northwestern corner of the Indian subcontinent, surrounded by its neighbors Iran, Afghanistan, China, and India. The country was created in 1947, when the Muslim-dominated northeastern and northwestern states of India were given autonomy at the end of British rule.

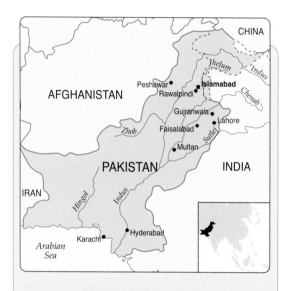

NATIONAL DATA – PAKISTAN

Land area   778,720 sq km (300,665 sq mi)

Climate	Altitude m (ft)	Temperatures January °C(°F)	July °C(°F)	Annual precipitation mm (in)
Islamabad	511 (1,644)	10 (50)	29 (84)	1,142 (44.9)
Karachi	4 (13)	20 (68)	30 (86)	168 (6.6)

Major physical features   highest point: K2 8,611 m (28,251 ft); longest river: Indus 2,896 km (1,800 mi)

Population   (2006 est.) 165,803,560

Form of government   federal multiparty republic with two legislative houses

Armed forces   army 550,000; navy 24,000; air force 45,000

Largest cities   Karachi (12,315,843); Lahore (6,659,543); Faisalabad (2,658,181); Rawalpindi (1,843,418); Multan (1,506,424); Gujranwala (1,459,139); Hyderabad (1,447,275); Islamabad (capital - 955,629)

Official languages   Urdu, English

Ethnic composition   Punjabi 48.2%; Pashto 13.1%; Sindhi 11.8%; Saraiki 9.8%; Urdu 7.6%; others 9.5%

Official religion   Islam

Religious affiliations   Muslim 97% (Sunni 77%, Shi'a 20%); Christian, Hindu, and other 3%

Currency   1 Pakistani rupee (PKR) = 100 paisa

Gross domestic product   (2006) U.S. $427.3 billion

Gross domestic product per capita   (2006) U.S. $2,600

Life expectancy at birth   male 62.4 yr; female 64.44 yr

Major resources   coal, cement, cotton, fertilizers, food processing, livestock, fisheries, petroleum, natural gas, sugarcane, yarn, fabric, iron ore, copper, salt, limestone

Geography

Rising in the Himalayas to the northeast, the Indus River drains the whole of Pakistan from the lofty northern plateaus to the southern plains. Along the frontier with Afghanistan, the Khyber Pass forms an irregular plateau in the foothills of the Himalayas. Farther south are the Punjab plains, the fertile heartland of Pakistan watered by the Indus and its tributaries. In the southwest is the arid plateau of Baluchistan.

The country has a continental climate with very hot summers and cool winters and large daily variations in temperature. Most of Pakistan's rain falls between July and September, when monsoon winds blow from the southwest. Vegetation grows only sparsely over much of the country. In the northwest there are forests of pine, deodar, and holly, while deciduous trees such as planes and poplar grow in the far north. The mountains are rich in wildlife, including bears, leopards, and wild sheep. However, forest cover has been reduced to a little over 3 percent of the land area, and animal habitats are under threat.

Society

During the creation of Pakistan part of Bengal in the northeastern part of India became East Pakistan, and part of Punjab in the west formed West Pakistan. In 1956 an Islamic republic was proclaimed. Two years later a military coup occurred. In 1965 disputes with India over the Kashmiri border erupted into war. During the elections of 1971 East Pakistan demanded independence, and in 1972, following a civil war in which India supported East Pakistan, that territory became the independent state of Bangladesh.

There followed a period of civilian rule by Zulfikar Ali Bhutto (1928–79), which ended in him being hanged for attempted murder. Following a period of martial law under General Zia-ul-Haq (1924–88), Bhutto's daughter, Benazir (b. 1953), was elected to power in 1999. She was imprisoned for corruption, and military rule was restored under General Pervez Musharraf (b. 1943). Pakistan has become a breeding ground and refuge for Islamic terrorists in recent years, but the government has pledged to help flush them out as part of its contribution to the war against terror.

GOVERNMENT AND PEOPLE

Pakistan has two legislative bodies: the national assembly, headed by the prime minister, and the senate, whose members are chosen by the four provincial assemblies. The president is head of state and commander of the armed forces. The people of Pakistan are racially mixed, the result of centuries of invasions and migrations. The main linguistic division is between Iranian languages (such as Baluchi and Pashto) and the Indo-Aryan group, which includes Punjabi, Sindhi, and the official language, Urdu. Islam is the official religion, and is followed by nearly 97 percent of the population.

Economy

The country faces an economic crisis with inadequate revenue, high unemployment, and insufficient foreign investment. Internal political upheavals and the costs of the ongoing dispute with India over Kashmir have also held back the economy. Poverty is widespread, with about 35 percent of the population living below the poverty line. The country relies on foreign aid and remittances from Pakistanis working abroad. Agriculture employs nearly half the workforce, although this accounts for less than one-quarter of national income. Livestock are numerous, but milk and meat yields are low because of a shortage of fodder. Fishing is a significant growth industry. Pakistan has some coal, oil, and metallic ores such as iron and copper. Limestone is the basis of the cement industry. The cotton industry developed rapidly after independence and is still important. Other products, including leather, wool, and sugar, are processed both for the home and export markets. Heavy industry is under government control.

The country's main road and rail routes link the principal seaport, Karachi, to Lahore, Islamabad, and Peshawar. Healthcare suffers from too few trained staff. There is only basic welfare provision. Primary education is free and widely available, but few receive further education. Literacy levels remain comparatively low.

Sacrificial animals gathered for a Muslim festival (Eid ul Adha) in the capital, Karachi.

INDIA

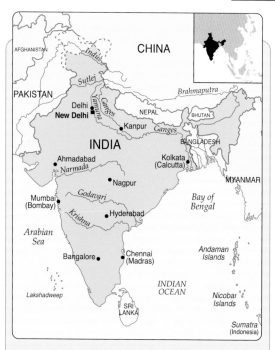

NATIONAL DATA – INDIA

Land area 2,973,190 sq km (1,147,955 sq mi)

Climate	Altitude m (ft)	Temperatures January °C(°F)	July °C(°F)	Annual precipitation mm (in)
New Delhi	216 (708)	14 (57)	30 (86)	797 (31.3)
Cherrapunji (near Shillong)	1,313 (4,309)	12 (54)	20 (68)	10,799 (425.1)
Chennai (Madras)	16 (51)	25 (77)	30 (86)	1,266 (49.8)

Major physical features highest point: Kanchenjunga 8,586 m (28,169 ft); longest rivers: Brahmaputra (part) 2,900 km (1,800 mi), Ganges 2,505 km (1,557 mi)

Population (2006 est.) 1,095,351,995

Form of government multiparty republic with two legislative houses

Armed forces army 1,100,000; navy 55,000; air force 170,000

Largest cities Mumbai/Bombay (13,073,926); New Delhi (capital – 11,505,196); Bangalore (5,281,927); Kolkata/Calcutta (4,643,011); Chennai/Madras (4,376,400); Ahmadabad (3,819,497); Hyderabad (3,665,106)

Official languages National: Hindi; English State: Bengali; Telugu; Marathi; Tamil; Urdu; Gujarati; Malayalani; Kannada; Oriya; Punjabi; Assamese; Kashmiri; Sindhi; Sanskrit

Ethnic composition Indo-Aryan 72%; Dravidian 25%; Mongoloid and other 3%

Religious affiliations Hindu 80.5%; Muslim 13.4%; Christian 2.3%; Sikh 1.9%; other 1.8%; unspecified 0.1%

Currency 1 Indian rupee (INR) = 100 paise

Gross domestic product (2006) U.S. $4.042 trillion

Gross domestic product per capita (2006) U.S. $3,700

Life expectancy at birth male 63.9 yr; female 65.57 yr

Major resources coal, iron ore, manganese, mica, bauxite, titanium ore, chromite, natural gas, diamonds, petroleum, limestone, tea, coffee, rubber, pepper, coconuts, jute, cotton, barley, fruit, gemstones, ground nuts, millet, potatoes, pulses, rice, sorghum, sugarcane, tea, vegetables, wheat, livestock

The Indian subcontinent is a large peninsula in southern Asia, covering an area about one-third the size of the United States. India boasts one of the world's oldest civilizations (the Aryans and the Dravidians), whose history has been traced to the 15th century B.C.

Geography

The varied landscapes are the result of plate tectonics— movements of continental landmasses. The massive Himalaya Mountains in the north and the great trench to the south of them were formed by the collision of two ancient continental "plates." The Himalayas, forming a barrier to the rest of Asia, descend southward to a fertile alluvial plain that crosses the country east to west. The rest of the Indian peninsula is bordered by coastal hills, the Eastern and Western Ghats.

In winter most places experience cold Himalayan winds, but the south and west remain hot and humid. After the spring, most regions are hot and dry, with only

The mighty Ganges River at Varanasi. The river flows southeast along the Indian plains toward the Bay of Bengal.

the monsoons bringing relief. In fall, cyclones are likely. Less than one-fifth of India is still forested. Most river deltas have mangrove forests on their seaward edges, and tropical forest is found on higher ground. In the wetter parts of the eastern Himalayas evergreen oak and chestnut, and rhododendrons, are common. India has a rich variety of wildlife, but as forests are cleared, habitats are lost. Protected species include Asian elephants, Indian rhinos, gaurs, Asiatic lions, tigers, snow leopards, great Indian bustards, and gharials.

Society

Since the first trace of a major civilization—in the Indus Valley in 2500 B.C.—the region has seen many different kingdoms established, each with a unique culture. European interest in the region began in the 16th

century, and by the 17th century the Dutch, French, and British had set up trading stations. By 1849 India had became part of the British Empire, but in the early 20th century nationalists had begun to question Britain's right to rule India. Years of civil disobedience, rioting, and bloodshed eventually led to India achieving independence in 1947. At the same time, partition brought about the Muslim state of Pakistan.

Society

The economy has improved in recent years, but there are regional imbalances. Investment by other countries has expanded, and foreign debt has declined. Reforms have brought a freer market economy, and the privatization of state enterprises continues. The region around Bangalore has seen the development of high-tech industries, and India is a leading exporter of software. India has many highly educated workers, and many British companies have established call centers there.

Agriculture occupies two-thirds of the workforce, with rice the main crop. India has the world's largest livestock population, but yields are low because of inadequate fodder. Massive iron ore deposits are exploited. There are also minerals such as oil and coal. Manufacturing is growing fast; products include textiles and electrical appliances. However, poverty and malnutrition are rife, and medical resources are overstretched. Despite birth control measures, India will soon overtake China as the most populous nation.

THE PEOPLE OF INDIA

India has a complex racial mix, and more than 700 languages and dialects exist. The largest group is the Indo-Aryan languages, spoken throughout northern and western India. India's dominant religion is Hinduism, but there are significant minorities of other religions. The caste system divides Hindus into 3,000 groups according to birthplace and occupation. Members of different castes cannot intermarry without one of them "losing caste." The lowest caste are the "untouchables." in 1997 Kocheril Roman Narayanan (1920–2005) was elected the first "untouchable" president.

SRI LANKA

The island state of Sri Lanka lies off the southeast coast of India. Once a popular tourist destination, in recent years it has been plunged into ethnic violence.

Geography

The Palk Strait, a narrow stretch of water, separates Sri Lanka from the southeastern coast of the Indian peninsula. The landscape is dominated by the central mountainous region, which rises to its highest point near the middle of the island at Pidurutalagala. Small rivers radiate from the highlands, cascading in waterfalls onto the plains below. The rest of the country is mainly lowlying, interrupted by steep ridges and by inselbergs—ancient eroded blocks of stone. The coast is partially fringed with coral islands and lagoons, particularly in the far northwest around the Jaffna Peninsula and Mannar Island. The country is hot and humid all year. From May to October the summer monsoon brings rain to most parts of the island. In fall some northern and eastern regions receive heavier rainfall. The monsoon is often unreliable, however, and severe droughts followed by floods are not uncommon.

Rich rain forests grow in the wetter areas, while hardier monsoon forests with valuable trees such as ebony and satinwood grow in drier regions. Much of Sri Lanka's forests have now been cleared. The island's

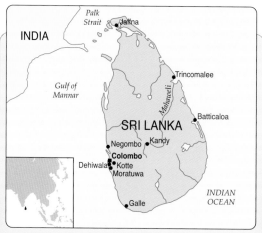

NATIONAL DATA – SRI LANKA

Land area	64,740 sq km (24,996 sq mi)			

Climate		Temperatures		Annual
	Altitude m (ft)	January °C(°F)	July °C(°F)	precipitation mm (in)
Colombo	7 (23)	27 (81)	27 (81)	2,524 (99.3)

Major physical features highest point: Pidurutalagala 2,524 m (8,281 ft); longest river: Mahaweli 332 km (206 mi)

Population (2006 est.) 20,222,240

Form of government multiparty republic with one legislative house

Armed forces army 78,000; navy 15,000; air force 18,000

Largest cities Colombo (capital - 650,875); Dehiwala (219,114); Moratuwa (189,155); Jaffna (172,812) (Kotte - legislative capital 119,364)

Official language Sinhala, Tamil

Ethnic composition Sinhalese 73.8%; Sri Lankan Moors 7.2%; Indian Tamil 4.6%; Sri Lankan Tamil 3.9%; other 0.5%; unspecified 10%

Religious affiliations Buddhist 69.1%; Muslim 7.6%; Hindu 7.1%; Christian 6.2%; unspecified 10%

Currency 1 Sri Lankan rupee (LKR) = 100 cents

Gross domestic product (2006) U.S. $93.33 billion

Gross domestic product per capita (2006) U.S. $4,600

Life expectancy at birth male 70.83 yr; female 76.12 yr

Major resources limestone, graphite, mineral sands, gems, phosphates, clay, hydropower, tea, rubber, coconuts, tourism, cassava, coconuts, fish, fruit, iron ore, rice, semi precious gemstones, spices, timber

elephant population is now down to a few hundred only. Other large animals found on the island include leopards, bears, jackals, wild pigs, and monkeys.

Society

The island was settled in about the 5th century B.C. by Sinhalese people from northern India who later established a Buddhist kingdom. From about 1200 A.D. Tamils from southern India founded a Hindu kingdom in the north. The Portuguese colonized the island in the 16th century, but the Sinhalese managed to maintain an independent mountain kingdom around Kandy.

The Portuguese were ousted by the Dutch, and in 1796 the island, which Europeans called Ceylon, became a British colony. Ceylon achieved dominion status in 1947. In 1960 Sirimavo Bandaranaike (1916-2000) became the world's first woman prime minister. Ceylon became the Republic of Sri Lanka in 1972, but the slide into economic decline continued. Ethnic violence flared up between the Tamils and the Sinhalese in the 1980s and still remains a smouldering issue. Both Tamil and Sinhalese communities have a caste system similar to the one in India. Throughout its history Sri Lankan society has retained its own religious faith and cultural identity. Generally, the Sinhalese are Buddhists, the Tamils are Hindus, and the Sri Lankan Moors practice Islam. There are also some Christians within most ethnic groups.

Economy

The unrest caused by the Tamils has damaged the tourist

A Sri Lankan tea plantation. In the background, a Hindu temple and settlement are reminders of the majority religion on the island.

industry as well as other parts of the economy. The tsunami that hit the region in December 2004 killed or displaced over half a million people and destroyed huge amounts of property. In the late 1990s plantation crops—mainly tea, rubber, and coconuts—contributed 20 percent of exports, but this figure has been steadily falling. About 28 percent of the workforce is employed in agriculture. The chief subsistence crop is rice, although harvests fall short of the country's needs. Fruit, vegetables, and spices are grown as staples and for export. Fishing is important, and reforestation has produced timber mainly for domestic use.

Industry employs some 17 percent of the workforce. Sri Lanka depends on hydroelectricity and imported oil to generate power. Graphite is mined and is a key export. Other minerals include iron ore, kaolin, and gemstones. Cement manufacturing and the construction industry utilize the limestone in the north. Textiles and garments account for about 60 percent of GDP.

The services employ about 45 percent of the workforce in activities such as telecommunications, banking, and insurance. Tourism is a big potential revenue earner. About 800,000 Sri Lankans work abroad and send remittances home. Sri Lanka has extensive road and railroad networks and national and international air services. Social welfare programs cater to unemployment, disability, and old age, but urban housing is insufficient. Medical care is free, but malnutrition and disease are both widespread.

BANGLADESH

Bangladesh is a small, densely populated country occupying the eastern two-thirds of the Ganges–Brahmaputra delta. The land is fertile but prone to severe flooding, especially in the monsoon season; a flood action plan aims to reduce this problem. The land is mostly flat plains crossed by rivers, and a huge mangrove swampland lies to the south. The flatness of the land is broken only in the northeast and southeast, where the Chittagong Hills run along the border with Myanmar. Less than 10 percent of the land is forested, but bamboo and rattan grow in the eastern forests, and fruit trees are cultivated in the inland areas of Bangladesh. The country's wildlife includes rare Bengal tigers, clouded leopards, and Asiatic elephants.

Known as East Pakistan at the time of partition in 1947 when British rule ended in India, the state of Bangladesh was formed in 1971 after it pressed for autonomy from West Pakistan (now Pakistan).

Bangladesh is one of the world's poorest countries and is heavily dependent on foreign aid; more NGOs operate in Bangladesh than in any other country. With a rapidly increasing population, there are more people entering the job market than there are jobs, and one-third of the workforce is unemployed. Money sent home from Bangladeshis working abroad is important.

Essentially an agrarian economy, it is subject to the vagaries of the climate; floods and droughts bring frequent famines. Rice is the main crop, but fishing is also important. With few minerals, the steel, chemical, and textile industries rely on imported raw materials, bought with aid. Industries using local resources include jute processing (for rope) and bamboo (for making paper). Welfare and education is provided by agencies and the government, but malnutrition is widespread.

In countries such as Bangladesh, rivers provide a free and convenient way of washing clothes before allowing them to dry in the sun.

NATIONAL DATA – BANGLADESH

Land area	133,910 sq km (51,703 sq mi)			

Climate	Altitude m (ft)	Temperatures January °C(°F)	July °C(°F)	Annual precipitation mm (in)
Dhaka	8 (26)	19 (66)	29 (78)	1,920 (75.5)

Major physical features longest river: Brahmaputra (part) 2,900 km (1,800 mi)

Population (2006 est.) 147,365,352

Form of government multiparty republic with one legislative house

Armed forces army 110,000; navy 9,000; air force 6,500

Largest cities Dhaka (capital – 6,969,458); Chittagong (3,920,222); Khulna (1,400,689); Rajshahi (727,083); Komilla (419,623); Tungi (368,914)

Official language Bangla (Bengali)

Ethnic composition Bengali 97.7%; Bihari 1.3%; others 1.0%

Religious affiliations Muslim 83%; Hindu 16%; Buddhist 0.6%; Christian 0.3%; others 0.4%

Currency 1 taka (BDT) = 100 paisa

Gross domestic product (2006) U.S. $330.8 billion

Gross domestic product per capita (2006) U.S. $2,200

Life expectancy at birth male 62.47 yr; female 62.45 yr

Major resources natural gas, sugarcane, tea, rice, cotton, jute, fisheries, timber, coal, cattle, glass sand, limestone, peat, salt, tobacco, wheat, white clay

NEPAL

A stupa (a monument to Buddha) with 6,812-m- (22,350-ft-) high
Ama Dablam in the background. This famous Nepalese peak
dominates the sky for several days on the trek to Mount Everest.

Nepal is a small landlocked kingdom in the eastern
Himalayas. The world's highest peak, Mount Everest,
is located in the north, beyond the Kathmandu Valley.
Southern Nepal is the birthplace of Buddha (563–438
B.C.), but today most Nepalese are Hindus. The climate
ranges from subtropical in the south to Alpine in the
north. More than half the country is forested, and the
Tarai Lowlands have tigers, leopards, and rhinos. Goats,
yaks, and snow leopards live above the treeline. Most
Nepalese are of Indian descent. The famous Gurkhas
are regularly recruited into the British Army.

A Maoist insurgency that threatens to bring down
the government has damaged an already struggling
economy. Nepal is one of the world's poorest and least
developed countries, and is reliant on foreign grants.
Most people live by subsistence farming. Mineral
resources are small in quantity. Manufacturing is mainly
based around the processing of agricultural products.

NATIONAL DATA – NEPAL

Land area   143,181 sq km (55,208 sq mi)

Climate		Temperatures		Annual
	Altitude m (ft)	January °C(°F)	July °C(°F)	precipitation mm (in)
Kathmandu	1,334 (4,376)	26 (79)	25 (77)	1,461 (57.5)

Major physical features   highest point: Mount Everest 8,850 m (29,035 ft);
longest river: Ghaghara (part) 915 km (570 mi)

Population   (2006 est.) 28,287,147

Form of government   multiparty constitutional monarchy with two legislative
houses

Armed forces   army 69,000

Capital city   Kathmandu (856,340)

Official language   Nepali

Ethnic composition   Chhettri 15.5%; Brahman-Hill 12.5%; Magar 7%; Tharu 6.6%;
Tamang 5.5%; Newar 5.4%; Muslim 4.2%; Kami 3.9%; Yadav 3.9%; other 32.7%;
unspecified 2.8%

Religious affiliations   Hindu 80.6%; Buddhist 10.7%; Muslim 4.2%; Kirant 3.6%;
other 0.9%

Currency   1 Nepalese rupee (NPR) = 100 paisa

Gross domestic product   (2006) U.S. $41.92 billion

Gross domestic product per capita   (2006) U.S. $1,500

Life expectancy at birth   male 60.43 yr; female 59.91 yr

Major resources   quartz, water, timber, hydropower, lignite, copper, cobalt,
iron ore, barley, cattle, fruit, jute, medicinal herbs, pepper, potatoes, rice,
sugarcane, tobacco, wheat

BHUTAN

Tiny Bhutan is sandwiched between Tibet (now occupied by China) and India, in the eastern Himalayas. Long isolated from the rest of the world, Bhutan remains a mysterious kingdom. It is a country of high mountains and deep valleys. From the lowlands on the southern border, the land rises sharply to rugged mountains and broad valleys. Above these tower even greater Himalayan peaks that run along the Tibetan border. The climate ranges from subtropical in the south to Alpine in the north. Most people live in the temperate central valleys, where there is seasonal pastureland. Bamboo forests and savanna predominate on the southern lowlands and slopes. Wildlife includes elephants, tigers and, in the mountains, yaks and tahrs.

A system of hereditary monarchy, the Dragon King, was installed by the British in 1907 and still operates today. However, in recent years it has faced severe unrest from those who want democratic reforms to be instigated. The government also expelled 100,00 Nepali-speaking Hindus to Nepal during demonstrations.

Agriculture, mostly at the subsistence level, is the mainstay of a small and underdeveloped economy and employs about 90 percent of the workforce. Rice, buckwheat, and potatoes are among the major crops. There is also some livestock rearing and forestry. The major mineral resource is coal, but other minerals are also mined. Manufacturing is not advanced technically, and consists chiefly of food, timber, and pulp products. Together with hydroelectricity, these are the main exports. Most trade is with India, which supplies much of the country's manufactured goods. Tourism has growth potential, but at present is strictly controlled. There are few roads in Bhutan. Welfare is free but unavailable to most people, and there is widespread illiteracy.

NATIONAL DATA – BHUTAN

Land area 47,000 sq km (18,147 sq mi)

Climate	Altitude m (ft)	Temperatures January °C(°F)	July °C(°F)	Annual precipitation mm (in)
Thimphu	2,265 (7,431)	4 (39)	17 (63)	3,000 (118)

Major physical features highest point: Kula Kangri 7,554 m (24,784 ft)

Population (2006 est.) 2,279,723

Form of government constitutional monarchy

Armed forces army 6,000

Capital city Thimphu (79,334)

Official language Dzongkha (a form of Tibetan)

Ethnic composition Bhote 50%; ethnic Nepalese 35% (includes Lhotsampas–one of many Nepalese ethnic groups); indigenous or migrant tribes 15%

Religious affiliations Lamaistic Buddhist 75%; Indian- and Nepalese-influenced Hinduism 25%

Currency 1 ngultrum (BTN) = 100 chetrum

Gross domestic product (2003) U.S. $2.9 billion

Gross domestic product per capita (2003) U.S. $1,400

Life expectancy at birth male 55.02 yr; female 54.53 yr

Major resources timber, hydropower, gypsum, calcium carbonate, apples, barley, cardamom, coal, corn, dolomite, maize/corn, millet, oranges, potatoes, rice, buckwheat, yaks

MALDIVES

The Maldives are a chain of about 19 island groups in the Indian Ocean. The islands are atolls—coral reefs surrounding the peaks of submerged volcanic mountains. The climate is mainly hot and humid. Nearby barrier reefs provide the only protection from occasional violent monsoon-related cyclones, but about 80 percent of the land is less than 1 m (3 ft) above sea level. Altogether there are some 2,000 islands, of which only about 200 are inhabited. Parts of the Maldives are indeed a tropical island paradise—set in an azure blue sea the islands are crowned with forests of breadfruit and palm trees, and they are ringed with sandy beaches and clear lagoons. The coral reefs surrounding the islands are home to a wide variety of marine life, including many species of fish, mollusks, and turtles.

The Maldives attained independence from Britain in 1965. Long-time president Maumoon Abdul Gayoom (b. 1937) has survived an attempted coup and riots in support of democratic reforms. Tourism accounts for 20 percent of GDP and more than 60 percent of foreign exchange. Fishing provides most other national income. Agriculture is only at a subsistence level and is constrained by a lack of suitable land. Crops include millet, cassava, and yams, and coconuts are gathered for food and copra. Industries consisting of garment manufacture, boat building, and handicrafts account for about 18 percent of GDP. Vital imports, chiefly from India, include food, manufactured goods, and fuel for energy. Transportation is mainly by boat and air.

An atoll in the Maldives, from the air. Although an idyllic tourist destination, the islands are very lowlying and highly vulnerable to inundation by tidal waves during tropical storms.

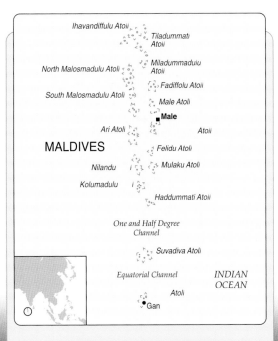

NATIONAL DATA - MALDIVES

Land area	300 sq km (116 sq mi)			
Climate		**Temperatures**		**Annual**
	Altitude m (ft)	**January** °C(°F)	**July** °C(°F)	**precipitation** mm (in)
Male	1 (3)	23 (73)	23 (73)	1,911 (75.2)

Population	(2006 est.) 359,008
Form of government	nonparty republic with one legislative house
Armed forces	army 900
Capital city	Male (89,287)
Official language	Divehi
Ethnic composition	Sinhalese, Dravidian, Arab, African
Official religion	Islam
Religious affiliations	Sunni Muslim 100%
Currency	1 rufiyaa (MVR) = 100 laari
Gross domestic product	(2002) U.S. $1.25 billion
Gross domestic product per capita	(2002) U.S. $3,900
Life expectancy at birth	male 63.08 yr; female 65.8 yr
Major resources	fisheries, tourism, coconuts/copra, fruit, vegetables

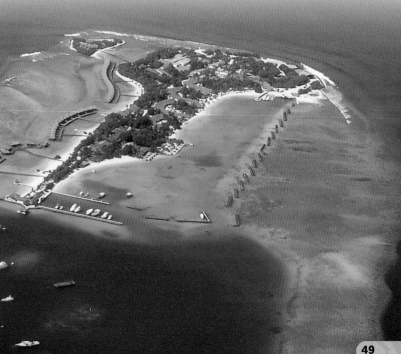

MYANMAR (ex BURMA)

Myanmar is the westernmost of the Southeast Asian countries. The land consists of a central lowland area enclosed by mountains to the east and west. To the north are more mountains—part of the Himalayas—which radiate southward in three great branches. The

The gold-leaf gilded Buddhist Shwezigon Pagoda in Bagan was completed in 1102. It is said to enshrine a bone and tooth of Buddha himself.

NATIONAL DATA – MYANMAR (ex-BURMA)

Land area   657,740 sq km (253,955 sq mi)

Climate		Temperatures		Annual
	Altitude m (ft)	January °C(°F)	July °C(°F)	precipitation mm (in)
Rangoon	23 (75)	26 (78)	27 (79)	2,731 (107.5)

Major physical features highest point: Mount Hkakabo 5,881 m (19,296 ft); longest river: Irrawaddy 2,092 km (1,300 mi)

Population (2006 est.) 47,382,633

Form of government military republic

Armed forces army 350,000; navy 13,000; air force 12,000

Largest cities Rangoon/Yangon (capital – 4,668,755); Mandalay (1,266,453); Mawlamyine (463,401); Bago (253,489); Pathein (246,228); Monywa (189,617)

Official language Burmese

Ethnic composition Burman 68%; Shan 9%; Karen 7%; Rakhine 4%; Chinese 3%; Indian 2%; Mon 2%; other 5%

Religious affiliations Buddhist 89%; Christian 4% (Baptist 3%; Roman Catholic 1%); Muslim 4%; animist 1%; other 2%

Currency 1 kyat (MMK) = 100 pyas

Gross domestic product (2006) U.S. $83.84 billion

Gross domestic product per capita (2006) U.S. $1,800

Life expectancy at birth male 58.07 yr; female 64.03 yr

Major resources petroleum, timber, tin, antimony, zinc, copper, tungsten, lead, coal, marble, limestone, precious stones, natural gas, hydropower, beans, chromium, cotton, groundnuts/peanuts, gold, gypsum, jute, nickel, pulses, cereals, rice, rubber, sugarcane

country has a tropical monsoon climate moderated by altitude. About half the land is still forested, and mangroves flourish in the coastal deltas. The wildlife includes elephants, tigers, rhinos, snakes, and monkeys.

A military government has held power since 1962, despite a multiparty election bringing victory to the opposition parties, whose leaders are either jailed or harassed. Rice has long been the country's major crop and chief export. Other crops include cereals, cotton, peanuts, and pulses. Forest hardwoods earn valuable foreign currency, as does the flourishing opium crop. Cattle are the main livestock. Myanmar's rich natural resources meet domestic needs. The country is also rich in rubies and sapphires. Petroleum and metal refining are major industries. Roads and railroads are mainly confined to central and southern lowlands; most goods are carried by water. Many people are still at the mercy of diseases such as malaria, polio, and cholera.

LAOS

Laos is the only landlocked state in Southeast Asia. It also has one of the smallest populations in the region. Northwestern Laos rises from the Mekong Valley lowlands to the Xieng Khouang Plateau. North and east of the plateau the landscape becomes extremely mountainous. In the southwest the Mekong River forms the border with Thailand. The monsoon season is generally hot and humid with heavy rainfall. More than half the land is covered by forest.

The first Lao peoples arrived from southwestern China in about the 8th century A.D. By 1907 it had become a French protectorate, with independence achieved in 1953. Conflict between the constitutional monarchy and the opposition Communist Pathet Lao movement escalated in the 1960s. The Communists gained power in 1975. Political parties are banned.

Agriculture employs more than three-quarters of the workforce, with rice the main crop. Opium has become an important unofficial cash crop; other crops are coffee, tobacco, and cotton. Forests yield hardwoods, oils, and spices. Although there are reserves of minerals, manufacturing is limited to processing raw materials. Since the mid-1980s the rigid communist economic system has been reformed, and private enterprise is encouraged. Western investment has also been welcomed. Most roads are unsurfaced, and there are few railroads. River traffic is the country's lifeline. Health conditions are poor, and life expectancy is low.

The village of Luang Nam Tha in Laos. Life is basic for the majority of Laotian peasants who derive much of their income from rice—the principal crop—which they grow on small, irrigated holdings.

NATIONAL DATA – LAOS

Land area	230,800 sq km (89,112 sq mi)			

Climate		Temperatures		Annual
	Altitude m (ft)	January °C(°F)	July °C(°F)	precipitation mm (in)
Vientiane	162 (531)	25 (77)	28 (82)	895 (35.2)

Major physical features highest point: Mount Bia 2,818 m (9,245 ft); longest river: Mekong (part) 4,200 km (2,600 mi)

Population (2006 est.) 6,368,481

Form of government one-party (Communist) republic with one legislative house

Armed forces army 25,600; air force 3,500

Capital city Vientiane (202,908)

Official language Lao

Ethnic composition Lao Loum (lowland) 68%; Lao Theung (upland) 22%; Lao Soung (highland) including the Hmong and the Yao 9%; ethnic Vietnamese/Chinese 1%

Religious affiliations Buddhist 60%; animist and other 40% (including various Christian denominations 1.5%)

Currency 1 kip (LAK) = 100 at

Gross domestic product (2006) U.S. $13.43 billion

Gross domestic product per capita (2006) U.S. $2,100

Life expectancy at birth male 53.45 yr; female 57.61 yr

Major resources timber, hydropower, gypsum, tin, gold, gemstones, rice, coffee, cotton, opium, spices, tobacco

VIETNAM

Vietnam is mainly mountainous. Central Vietnam is dominated by the rugged Annam Mountains. To the east lies a narrow coastal plain and at either end are sprawling flood plains, formed by the Red River delta and the Mekong River delta. These fertile rice-growing plains are the most populated region. The country has a tropical monsoon climate with much local variation. Tropical forests cover two-fifths of the country, but massive deforestation—to provide hardwood for foreign currency—has caused environmental damage. Elephants, tigers, bears, and other animals are found, but many are under threat from hunting and habitat destruction.

Vietnam has experienced centuries of foreign occupation, war, and partition. The country was reunified under Communist rule in 1975 after the Vietnam War (1959–75), but devastation, homelessness, natural disasters, and poor government have impeded progress. Agriculture employs most of the workforce, with rice the main crop and staple. Fish is also a staple. Industry includes steel and cement manufacture, food processing, and textiles. Road and railroads are poor, and the terrain hinders transport. Waterways are a major link. Health and welfare are improving.

Monolithic limestone islands covered with dense vegetation rise spectacularly from the sea in Halong Bay in the Gulf of Tonkin on the northern coast of Vietnam.

NATIONAL DATA – VIETNAM

Land area 325,360 sq km (125,622 sq mi)

Climate	Altitude m (ft)	Temperatures January °C(°F)	July °C(°F)	Annual precipitation mm (in)
Hanoi	16 (52)	17 (63)	29 (84)	1,667 (65.6)

Major physical features highest point: Fan-si-pan 3,141 m (10,306 ft); longest rivers: Mekong (part) 4,200 km (2,600 mi); Red (part) 805 km (500 mi)

Population (2006 est.) 84,402,966

Form of government one-party communist republic with one legislative house

Armed forces army 412,000; navy 13,000; air force 30,000

Largest cities Ho Chi Minh City (3,525,282); Hanoi (capital – 1,472,717); Haiphong (620,936); Da Nang (485,147)

Official language Vietnamese

Ethnic composition Kinh (Viet) 86.2%; Tay 1.9%; Thai 1.7%; Muong 1.5%; Khome 1.4%; Hoa 1.1%; Nun 1.1%; Hmong 1%; others 4.1%

Religious affiliations Buddhist 9.3%; Catholic 6.7%; Hoa Hao 1.5%; Cao Dai 1.1%; Protestant 0.5%; Muslim 0.1%; none 80.8%

Currency 1 dong (VND) = 10 hao = 100 xu

Gross domestic product (2006) U.S. $258.6 billion

Gross domestic product per capita (2006) U.S. $3,100

Life expectancy at birth male 68.05 yr; female 73.85 yr

Major resources phosphates, coal, manganese, bauxite, chromate, offshore oil and gas deposits, hydropower, anthracite, bananas, cassava, cattle, coffee, fisheries, gold, iron, lignite, limestone, maize/corn, pigs, pineapples, rice, rubber, salt, sweet potatoes, tea, timber, titanium, tobacco

CAMBODIA

Cambodia is a mainly lowland country. Tonle Sap (the Great Lake) at the heart of the country lies west of a wide alluvial plain fed by the Mekong River. Southwest of Tonle Sap, the Cardamom and Elephant Mountains overlook a narrow coastal plain. The climate is generally hot, with high humidity and rainfall in the monsoon season. About 70 percent of Cambodia is covered by forest—from broadleaf evergreens and deciduous woodlands in the north to tropical rain forests on mountains overlooking the sea. Lowland areas have open forest with savanna; paddies, reeds,

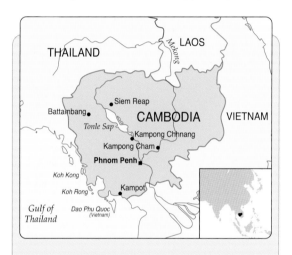

NATIONAL DATA – CAMBODIA

Land area 176,520 sq km (68,155 sq mi)				
Climate		Temperatures		Annual
	Altitude m (ft)	January °C(°F)	July °C(°F)	precipitation mm (in)
Phnom Penh	12 (39)	27 (81)	29 (84)	1,536 (60.4)

Major physical features   highest point: Mount Aôral 1,813 m (5,949 ft); longest river: Mekong (part) 4,200 km (2,600 mi); largest lake: Tonle Sap 2,590 to 24,605 sq km (1,000 to 9,500 sq mi) depending on the season

Population   (2006 est.) 13,881,427

Form of government   multiparty democracy under a constitutional monarchy

Armed forces   army 75,000; navy 2,800; air force 1,500

Capital city   Phnom Penh (1,781,113)

Official language   Khmer

Ethnic composition   Khmer 90%; Vietnamese 5%; Chinese 1%; other 4%

Religious affiliations   Theravada Buddhist 95%; other 5%

Currency   1 riel (KHR) = 100 sen

Gross domestic product   (2006) U.S. $36.78 billion

Gross domestic product per capita   (2006) U.S. $2,600

Life expectancy at birth   male 57.35 yr; female 61.32 yr

Major resources   oil, natural gas, timber, gemstones, iron ore, manganese, phosphates, hydropower potential, bananas, bauxite, cotton, fisheries, jute, livestock, maize/corn, pepper, rice, rubber, sugar palms, tobacco

Angkor Wat ("temple city") near Siem Reap is part of the ruins of the great Khmer civilization that ruled northwest Cambodia and eastern Thailand for 500 years until the 15th century.

and bamboo forest occur in wetter floodplains by rivers. Animals include elephants, tigers, bears, and leopards, and many waterbirds along the rivers.

One of the poorest states in the region, Cambodia suffered by aiding North Vietnam in the Vietnam War (1959–75). In 1975 the left-wing Khmer Rouge under Pol Pot (1925–98) ousted the pro-U.S. government and began a brutal ruralization of the entire society, in which two million people died. With the Khmer Rouge long gone, a more stable political situation exists.

Cambodia's economy is based on its rice crop—rice fields account for nearly 90 percent of arable land. Most people live and work as subsistence farmers. Fruit and livestock are among the other agricultural commodities. Large stocks of freshwater fish are taken from Tonle Sap. Manufacturing is confined to local processing of rubber and wood, and agricultural products. Few roads are surfaced, and many areas have no roads. Healthcare is improving, but diseases such as cholera and malaria are not under control, and malnutrition is common.

THAILAND

Known as Siam until 1939, Thailand is at the heart of the Indochinese peninsula in Southeast Asia. It has been an independent kingdom for many centuries, and although never colonized, it has not escaped foreign cultural and political influences, both from its neighbors and from the West. Today, Thailand maintains strong links with bordering countries as well as the West.

NATIONAL DATA – THAILAND

Land area	511,770 sq km (197,596 sq mi)			

Climate		Temperatures		Annual
	Altitude m (ft)	January °C(°F)	July °C(°F)	precipitation mm (in)
Bangkok	2 (7)	27 (81)	29 (84)	1,498 (58.9)

Major physical features highest point: Mount Inthanon 2,585 m (8,481 ft); longest river: Mekong (part) 4,200 km (2,600 mi)

Population (2006 est.) 64,631,595

Form of government multiparty constitutional monarchy

Armed forces army 190,000; navy 70,600; air force 46,000

Largest cities Bangkok (capital – 4,819,253); Nonthaburi (404,805); Samut Prakan (393,217); Udon Thani (255,754); Chon Buri (228,227); Nakhon Ratchasima (209,458)

Official language Thai

Ethnic composition Thai 75%, Chinese 14%, other 11%

Religious affiliations Buddhist 94.6%, Muslim 4.6%, Christian 0.7%, other 0.1%

Currency 1 baht (THB) = 100 satang

Gross domestic product (2006) U.S. $585.9 billion

Gross domestic product per capita (2006) U.S. $9,100

Life expectancy at birth male 69.95 yr; female 74.68 yr

Major resources tin, rubber, natural gas, tungsten, tantalum, timber, lead, gypsum, lignite, fluorite, maize/corn, rice, soybeans, sugarcane, cassava, sorghum, tea, tobacco, jute, livestock, fisheries, tourism, textiles

Geography

Thailand is a country of high mountains, rain forests, broad floodplains, and sandy beaches. The highest land is in the far north—the last bastion of the Himalayas. Mountains also run southward along the Myanmar border and down the southwestern isthmus. The east coast is gentler, with numerous sandy bays. Both coasts are fringed with beautiful islands. The most densely populated area is the fertile central plains of the Chao River delta, where most agricultural and commercial activities are concentrated. However, this area suffers from regular flooding. Eastern Thailand is made up of the Khorat Plateau, a landscape of rolling hills.

The country has a tropical monsoon climate. Generally, rainfall is lightest in the northeast and heaviest in the south and over the mountains. Much of the natural forest cover has been cleared for agriculture, and less than one-third of the original forest remains—mostly in the inaccessible northern areas. Hardwoods predominate. Game hunting has reduced the wildlife considerably. Leopards and tigers are now rare, and rhinos and tapirs are almost extinct.

Society

The Thai people are thought to have arrived from China about 1,000 years ago. Then followed the empire of the Sukhothai in the 13th century and the Buddhist kingdom of Ayutthaya. A Burmese victory in 1767 ended Ayutthaya rule, but the Burmese were ousted by the Chakkri dynasty, which has continued to the present day. Under this rule, Thailand broadened links with the West and abolished slavery. A bloodless coup in 1932 brought in a constitutional monarchy. In alliance with Japan in World War II, Thailand became a U.S. ally after the war. More recently, political instability has been caused by wars in neighboring lands, a military coup, guerrilla activity in border areas, and an influx of refugees.

THE PEOPLE OF THAILAND

Most of the population are ethnic Thais, including about 27 percent who are of Laotian origin. The large Chinese population lives mainly in the urban areas, whereas people of Malay ancestry—who practice Islam—are concentrated mainly in the south. The northern hills are inhabited by half a million non-Thai peoples, such as the Karen, the Meo Lahu, and the Akha. The vast majority of the population is Buddhist, and Thai culture reflects this in its ornamental temples and religious art and in the popular festivals that accompany religious and royal ceremonies.

Economy

Thailand achieved high commercial growth rates in the 1980s and 1990s, making it one of the boom economies in the Pacific rim region. Manufacturing, based on cheap labor (although living standards are rising), is expanding and includes textiles, clothing, plastics, and electrical and

A waterside village near Phang Nga Bay, Phuket. The sheer limestone cliffs rising from the sea are characteristic of the region.

electronic goods. Trade and manufacturing now employ about one-quarter of the workforce. Services, including tourism, make the largest contribution to GDP, however.

In December 2004 a tsunami took 8,500 lives and caused devastation to several provinces, damaging tourism and other industries. Around half the workforce is engaged in agriculture, most of them working in the country's extensive paddy fields. Rice is the chief staple and principal export crop. The hill people of the north have traditionally grown poppies for opium, but tobacco and tea are also grown. Cattle and buffalo are used mainly as draft animals, while pigs and poultry are reared for meat. Fish from both sea and freshwater form a major part of the Thai diet. Railroads are well developed, but roads are often inadequate. All transportation systems radiate from Bangkok. Social welfare is generally poor. Despite government help, there are still many major health problems.

MALAYSIA

Malaysia consists of West Malaysia on the Southeast Asian mainland and East Malaysia—comprising two states, Sabah and Sarawak—on the island of Borneo. Northern and central West Malaysia are mountainous, but the southeast has broad river valleys and coastal plains. In East Malaysia the mountains rise to their highest point at Mount Kinabalu. Both parts of Malaysia have a similar equatorial climate. There is rich animal and

NATIONAL DATA – MALAYSIA

Land area   328,550 sq km (126,854 sq mi)

Climate	Altitude m (ft)	Temperatures January °C(°F)	July °C(°F)	Annual precipitation mm (in)
Kuala Lumpur	39 (128)	27 (81)	28 (82)	2,431 (95.7)

Major physical features highest point: Mount Kinabalu 4,101 m (13,455 ft); longest river: Rajang (Borneo) 565 km (350 mi)

Population (2006 est.) 24,385,858

Form of government federal multiparty constitutional monarchy with two legislative houses

Armed forces army 80,000; navy 15,000; air force 15,000

Largest cities Kuala Lumpur (capital – 1,509,699); Subang Jaya (1,091,600); Klang (995,926)

Official language Bahasa Malaysian

Ethnic composition Malay 50.4%; Chinese 23.7%; Indigenous 11%; Indian 7.1%; others 7.8%

Official religion Islam

Religious affiliations Muslim 52.9%; Buddhist 17.3%; Chinese folk religions 11.6%; Hindu 7%; Christian 6.4%; others 4.8%

Currency 1 ringgit (MYR) = 100 sen

Gross domestic product (2006) U.S. $308.8 billion

Gross domestic product per capita (2006) U.S. $12,700

Life expectancy at birth male 69.8 yr; female 75.38 yr

Major resources tin, petroleum, timber, copper, iron ore, natural gas, bauxite, cocoa, fish, palm oil, pepper, pineapples, rice, rubber

The Petronas Twin Towers in Kuala Lumpur. At the time of its completion (1998), it was the tallest building in the world and a symbol of growing Malaysian influence and power.

plant life in the dense rain forests, including sun bears and orangutans.

Malaysia's economy is one of the strongest in Southeast Asia. Farming and forestry occupy about one-third of the workforce. The main crop is rubber, of which Malaysia is the world's leading supplier. It is a leading tin producer and has other resources such as petroleum, bauxite, and copper. Manufacturing includes electronic components for export alongside rubber goods and petroleum products. On the peninsula roads and railroads are well developed, but in East Malaysia rivers are the best means of communication.

SINGAPORE

Lying off the coast of Malaysia, Singapore is one of the most densely populated and most prosperous nations in the world. The majority of the population lives on Singapore Island, and the rest inhabits 54 nearby islets. Singapore Island has a low, undulating landscape with a hillier central area. The climate is uniformly hot and humid all year around, with high rainfall. Animal life includes the crab-eating macaque, a type of monkey.

Modern Singapore was founded in 1819 by Sir Thomas Raffles (1781–1826) of the British East India Company and later became a crown colony. This legacy is evident in the many gracious colonial buildings that sit side by side with new international hotels, shopping complexes, and office blocks in the commercial heart of the city. In 1963 Singapore was incorporated into the Federation of Malaysia but left two years later to become an independent republic. The head of state is a directly elected president. The three main ethnic groups—Chinese, Malay, and Indian—speak a variety of languages and practice various religions.

Agriculture and fisheries are relatively unimportant; many staple foods, including fish, are imported. The prosperous and expanding manufacturing sector is based on imported raw materials and employs about 18 percent of the workforce. Major industries include petrochemicals, textiles, and shipbuilding. Financial services, banking, and tourism are also major foreign currency earners, occupying about 40 percent of the workforce. There are road and rail links to neighboring parts of Malaysia, and a busy international airport. Singapore's port is one of the world's busiest in terms of tonnage handled. Healthcare, welfare, and education are all of a high standard.

Orchard Road in Singapore—a typical modern street with wide walkways—and an absence of litter that is one of the government's hallmarks.

NATIONAL DATA – SINGAPORE

Land area	683 sq km (264 sq mi)			
Climate		**Temperatures**		**Annual**
	Altitude m (ft)	January °C(°F)	July °C(°F)	precipitation mm (in)
Singapore	10 (33)	27 (81)	28 (82)	2,315 (91.1)

Major physical features largest island: Singapore 541 sq km (209 sq mi); highest point: Timah Hill 162 m (531 ft)

Population (2006 est.) 4,492,150

Form of government multiparty republic with one legislative house

Armed forces army 50,000; navy 4,000; air force 13,500

Capital city Singapore (3,654,103)

Official languages Chinese, Malay, Tamil, English

Ethnic composition Chinese 76.8%; Malay 13.9%; Indian 7.9%; other 1.4%

Religious affiliations Buddhist 42.5%; Muslim 14.9%; Taoist 8.5%; Hindu 4%; Catholic 4.8%; other Christian 9.8%; other 0.7%; none 14.8%

Currency 1 Singapore dollar (SGD) = 100 cents

Gross domestic product (2006) U.S. $138.6 billion

Gross domestic product per capita (2006) U.S. $30,900

Life expectancy at birth male 79.13 yr; female 84.49 yr

Major resources fisheries, deepwater ports, shipbuilding, financial services, tourism

BRUNEI

Brunei is an independent sultanate situated on the northwest coast of Borneo, and surrounded and divided in two by the Malaysian state of Sarawak. Both parts of Brunei share a landscape of hills and valleys bordering a narrow and often swampy coastal plain. The smaller eastern enclave is more rugged. The humid tropical climate brings heavy monsoon rains and encourages dense tropical forest, rich in hardwoods. Inaccessibility makes it a haven for wildlife such as monkeys, apes, and birds. Borneo became a British protectorate in 1888, and in 1929 the first petroleum reserves were discovered. The country achieved full independence within the Commonwealth in 1984, and since then political power has been vested in the sultan. Brunei has the lowest and least dense population of any Southeast Asian country.

Petroleum is the mainstay of the Brunei economy, enabling the country to enjoy one of the highest per capita incomes in Southeast Asia and making the sultan one of the world's richest people. In addition to petroleum, there are also reserves of natural gas. Other income derives from small-scale agriculture (pepper and rice are grown) and forestry (which produces cork and rubber). Most of the country's transportation links are along the coast and rivers, except for some coastal roads. Healthcare is good and free, even in isolated communities. Education also extends to remote areas.

The National Mosque of Brunei was completed in 1958. It is also known as the Omar Ali Saifuddien Mosque after the 28th sultan, who is regarded as the architect of modern Brunei.

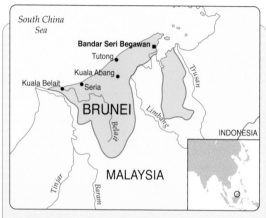

NATIONAL DATA – BRUNEI

Land area	5,270 sq km (2,035 sq mi)			

Climate	Altitude m (ft)	Temperatures January °C(°F)	July °C(°F)	Annual precipitation mm (in)
Bandar Seri Begawan	27 (80)	27 (81)	27 (81)	2,913 (114.6)

Major physical features   highest point: Pagon Peak 1,850 km (6,070 ft)

Population   (2006 est.) 379,444

Form of government   nonparty constitutional monarchy with one advisory body

Armed forces   army 4,900; navy 1,000; air force 1,100

Capital city   Bandar Seri Begawan (69,984)

Official language   Malay

Ethnic composition   Malay 67%; Chinese 15%; indigenous 6%; other 12%

Official religion   Islam

Religious affiliations   Muslim 67%; Buddhist 13%; Christian 10%; traditional beliefs and other 10%

Currency   1 Bruneian dollar (BND) = 100 cents

Gross domestic product   (2003) U.S. $6.842 billion

Gross domestic product per capita   (2003) U.S. $23,600

Life expectancy at birth   male 72.57 yr; female 77.59 yr

Major resources   petroleum, natural gas, rubber, timber, bananas, cassava, coffee, cork, fisheries, rice, pepper

PHILIPPINES

The Republic of the Philippines lies 800 km (500 mi) off the southeast coast of Asia and comprises an archipelago of 7,107 islands. It is in a region of tectonic instability—the "ring of fire"—that surrounds the Pacific Ocean, and in the path of violent storms. The islands are generally mountainous with narrow coastal plains, and some have dense populations. Vegetation ranges from tropical rain forest near the coasts to subtropical evergreens and pinewoods on the slopes, although many areas have been cleared. Geographical isolation has encouraged the evolution of many unique animals among the country's rich wildlife.

Most of today's Filipinos are of Mongoloid origin whose ancestors came from Taiwan and surrounding areas. Over time, intermingling with Chinese immigrants and Spanish and American colonists has taken place.

The country has an expanding economy using cheap labor, and farming and industry have also both benefited from investment and tax concessions. The country is largely agricultural, with rice the main crop. Manufacturing—often foreign owned—includes electronics, textiles, clothing, chemicals, and machinery.

NATIONAL DATA - PHILIPPINES

Land area	298,170 sq km (115,124 sq mi)			

Climate		Temperatures		Annual precipitation
	Altitude m (ft)	January °C(°F)	July °C(°F)	mm (in)
Manila	15 (49)	27 (75)	28 (82)	2,131 (83.8)

Major physical features largest island: Luzon 108,171 sq km (41,765 sq mi); highest point: Mount Apo (Mindanao) 2,954 m (9,692 ft)

Population (2006 est.) 89,468,677

Form of government multiparty republic with two legislative houses

Armed forces army 66,000; navy 24,000; air force 16,000

Largest cities Manila (capital - 10,665,584); Davao (1,278,148); Cebu (829,023); Antipolo (582,896)

Official languages Filipino, English

Ethnic composition Tagalog 28.1%; Cebuano 13.1%; Ilocano 9%; Bisaya/Binisaya 7.6%; Hiligaynon Ilonggo 7.5%; Bikol 6%; Waray 3.4%; other 25.3%

Religious affiliations Roman Catholic 80.9%; Evangelical 2.8%; Iglesia ni Kristo 2.3%; Aglipayan 2%; other Christian 4.5%; Muslim 5%; other 1.8%; unspecified 0.6%; none 0.1%

Currency 1 Philippine peso (PHP) = 100 centavos

Gross domestic product (2006) U.S. $443.1 billion

Gross domestic product per capita (2006) U.S. $5,000

Life expectancy at birth male 67.32 yr; female 73.24 yr

Major resources timber, petroleum, nickel, cobalt, silver, gold, salt, copper, coconuts, copra, fisheries, tobacco, rice, sugarcane, fruit

Hong Kong

Hong Kong is a small but very prosperous former British colony on the south coast of China, east of the Zhu River estuary. It consists of Hong Kong Island and the Kowloon Peninsula. To the north lie the more rural New Territories, and there are more than 230 nearby islands. The area is part of a semisubmerged mountain chain. Hong Kong has a subtropical monsoon climate; summers are hot and humid, and winters are relatively cool and dry. Most of the natural forest has been cleared, but some new woodland has been planted.

British merchants first arrived in the area in 1821, and by 1898 Hong Kong, Kowloon, and the New Territories had all been leased to Britain. In 1949 the region received a massive influx of Chinese nationals—many of them industrialists from Shanghai—escaping from communist China. A center for trade and finance, this former capitalist enclave was returned to communist China in 1997 as a special administrative region. At that time, it was agreed that the economic and social systems would remain intact for 50 years. Legislative Council elections in 1995 were won conclusively by pro-democracy parties, clearly indicating the future wishes of the population. The majority of the 7.3 million people is ethnic Chinese, but British influence has created a culture combining both Chinese and Western elements.

Hong Kong is the world's third largest financial center. Manufacturing includes textiles and electronic equipment. It is also Asia's premier tourist destination. Hong Kong has one of the world's largest container ports, and a new international airport was opened in 1998. The world's longest road and rail bridge, Tsing Ma Bridge, links the airport with Kowloon. With housing space at a premium there is little agricultural land, but fishing is well developed. Education and health are well maintained but there is little welfare provision.

Macao

Macao is a small special administrative region on China's south coast, facing west toward Hong Kong. It comprises a narrow mainland peninsula and two small islands: Taipa and Colôane. Both the peninsula and the islands have hilly interiors and outlying

flatlands. There are no rivers, and water must be imported from China or collected during the heavy rain that falls in the hot, humid summer monsoon season. The original forest has long since been cleared, but there is some reforestation at Colôane.

In 1557 the Portuguese leased Macao from China as a trade center and supply station. It flourished for many years, but in the mid-19th century it declined as Hong Kong grew in importance. In 1961 Macao became a Portuguese overseas province, but in 1999 it reverted to China. Macao has a population of about 450,000, most of whom live in the mainland peninsula area, which measures 6.5 sq km (2 sq mi). Portuguese is the official language, but most people are Chinese and speak a Cantonese dialect. There is little farmland in Macao, and few resources other than fish. It depends for its prosperity on its status as a free port and on exports

The swirling pattern of street tiles surrounding the central fountain are a popular landmark in Macao's Largo do Senado, or Senate Square.

of clothing, toys, and other consumer-based products. Tourism is also important, and Macao attracts millions each year with its casinos, historic buildings, and cheap consumer goods. The 64-km- (40-mi-) long Macao–Hong Kong sea route is one of the busiest in the world, with regular ferry, jetfoil, and hydrofoil services between the two territories. There are also air services, and a new international airport opened in 1999.

Christmas Island

Christmas Island lies about 400 km (250 mi) south of the western end of Java in the Indian Ocean. It covers an area of approximately 142 sq km (55 sq mi). The coast has steep cliffs, rising inland to a central plateau. The climate is tropical, with a wet season and a dry season. Most of the land is covered in tropical rain forest, and a large part of the island is designated as a National Park. The island was annexed by Britain in 1888, and the mining of phosphates began soon afterward in the 1890s. During World War II Christmas Island was held by the Japanese, but sovereignty passed to Australia in 1958. About 1,500 mainly ethnic Chinese and Europeans live on the island today. Phosphate mining is the main activity, but there are plans to build a space-launching site on the island.

Cocos (Keeling) Islands

This isolated group of coral islands some 36 sq km (14 sq mi) in area lies in the Indian Ocean, about 1,000 km (620 mi) southwest of Java. They were discovered in 1609 by William Keeling (1578–1620), a captain in the East India Company. In 1826 Englishman Alexander Hare established a small colony on the islands. The following year Scotsman John Clunies-Ross (1786–1854) brought a number of Malays to the islands and formed a second colony.

The two main atolls, also known as the Keeling Islands, were covered in coconut palms, which Clunies-Ross harvested for copra. Hare returned to Java in 1831, but Clunies-Ross remained on the islands, and they were controlled by his descendants until 1978. Although the islands were annexed to the British crown in 1857, Queen Victoria (1819–1901) returned them to the heirs of Clunies-Ross in perpetuity in 1886. Crown interests were later administered from Singapore and Ceylon (now Sri Lanka), but in 1955 authority passed to the Australian government. In 1978 Australia bought up the Clunies-Ross's interest—apart from the family home and grounds—and the islands became an external territory. The climate is tropical, with high humidity.

Of the 27 or so islands, only the two largest—West Island and Home Island—are inhabited. Today the copra harvest—the chief source of income—is gathered in by the descendants of the original laborers, who number about 600. Some small-scale farming (mainly vegetables, bananas, pawpaws, and coconuts), fishing, construction, and tourism also bring income to the islanders.

GLOSSARY

Words in SMALL CAPITALS refer to other entries in the Glossary.

Amerindian A member of one of the many INDIGENOUS PEOPLES of Central and South America.

Anglican A member of the PROTESTANT church— founded in England in the 16th century— including the Church of England and other churches throughout the world.

apartheid A way of organizing society to keep racial groups apart. Introduced after 1948 in South Africa by the National Party to ensure continued white political dominance, it has now been dismantled.

Buddhism A religion founded in India in the 6th and 5th centuries B.C. and based on the teachings of Gautama Siddhartha (c. 563–483 B.C.), the Buddha, or "Awakened One."

cereal A cultivated grass selectively bred to produce high yields of edible grain for consumption by humans and livestock. The most important are wheat (*Triticum*), rice (*Oryza sativa*), and maize/corn (*Zea mays*).

Christianity A religion based on the teachings of Jesus Christ and originating from JUDAISM in the 1st century A.D. Its main beliefs are found in the Bible, and it is now the world's most widespread religion, divided into a number of churches and sects, including ROMAN CATHOLICISM, PROTESTANTISM, and ORTHODOX CHURCHES.

Communism A social and economic system based on the communal ownership of property. It usually refers to the STATE-controlled social and economic systems in the former Soviet Union and Soviet bloc countries and in the People's Republic of China.

Confucianism A religion or moral code based on the teachings of the Chinese philosopher Confucius (c. 551–479 B.C.) that formed the foundations of Chinese imperial administration and ethical behavior; also followed in Korea and other east Asian countries.

constitution The fundamental statement of laws that defines the way a country is governed.

constitutional monarchy A form of government with a hereditary head of STATE or monarch and a CONSTITUTION.

democracy A form of government in which policy is made by the people (direct democracy) or on their behalf (indirect democracy). Indirect democracy usually takes the form of competition among political parties at elections.

Dependency (1) A territorial unit under the jurisdiction of another STATE but not formally annexed to it. **(2)** An unequal economic or political relationship between two states or groups of states, in which one side is dependent on and supports the other.

ethnic group A group of people sharing a social or cultural identity based on language, religion, customs and/or common descent or kinship.

EU (European Union) An alliance of European NATIONS formed to agree common policies in the areas of trade, aid, agriculture, and economics.

exports Goods or services sold to other countries.

federalism A form of CONSTITUTIONAL government in which power is shared between two levels—a central, or federal, government and a tier of provincial or STATE governments.

GDP (Gross Domestic Product) The total value of a country's annual output of goods and services with allowances made for depreciation.

Hinduism A religion originating in India in the 2nd millennium B.C. It emphasizes mystical contemplation and ascetic practices that are closely interwoven with much of Indian culture.

indigenous peoples The original inhabitants of a region.

Islam A religion based on the revelations of God to the prophet Muhammad in the 7th century A.D., as recorded in the Qu'ran. It teaches submission to the will of God and is practiced throughout the Middle East, North Africa, and parts of Southeast Asia.

Judaism A religion that developed in ancient Israel based on God's law and revelations declared to Moses on Mount Sinai.

Methodism A PROTESTANT denomination of the CHRISTIAN church based on the teachings of the English theologian John Wesley (1703–91).

monarch A form of rule where there is a hereditary head of STATE.

Muslim An adherent of ISLAM.

nation A community that believes it consists of a single people, based on historical and cultural criteria.

nation-state A STATE in which the inhabitants all belong to one NATION. Most states claim to be nation-states; in practice almost all of them include minority groups.

Native American The INDIGENOUS PEOPLES of North America.

official language The language used by governments, schools, courts, and other official institutions in countries where the population has no single common mother tongue.

one-party state A political system in which there is no competition to the government party at elections, as in COMMUNIST and military regimes.

parliamentary democracy A political system in which the legislature (Parliament) is elected by all the adult members of the population and the government is formed by the party that commands a majority in the Parliament.

Protestant Term describing CHRISTIAN denominations that share a common rejection of the authority of the pope as head of the church, and of many ROMAN CATHOLIC practices.

Roman Catholic The largest of the CHRISTIAN churches, headed by the pope in Rome. It traces its origin and authority to St. Peter, one of the disciples of Jesus Christ and the first bishop of Rome. There are believers on all continents.

Shi'ite Muslim A member of the smaller of the two main divisions of ISLAM. Followers recognize Muhammad's son-in-law, Ali, and his descendants, the imams (prayer leaders), as his true successors and legitimate leaders of Islam.

state The primary political unit of the modern world, usually defined by its possession of sovereignty over a territory and its people.

subtropical The climatic zone between the TROPICS and TEMPERATE zones. There are marked seasonal changes of temperature but it is never very cold.

Sunni Muslim A member of the larger of the two main divisions of ISLAM. Its members recognize the Caliphs as the successors to Muhammad and follow the *sunna*, or way of the prophet, as recorded in the *hadithw*, the teachings of Muhammad.

temperate climate Any one of the climatic zones in mid-latitudes, with a mild climate. They cover areas between the warm TROPICS and cold polar regions.

tropics (tropical) The area between the Tropic of Cancer (23°30'N) and the Tropic of Capricorn (23°30'S), marking the lines of latitude farthest from the equator where the Sun is still found directly overhead at midday in midsummer.

FURTHER REFERENCES

General Reference Books

Allen, J. L., *Student Atlas of World Geography*, McGraw-Hill, Columbus, OH, 2004.

Atlas of World Geography, Rand McNally, Chicago, IL, 2005.

Baines, J. D., Egan, V., and G. Bateman, *The Encyclopedia of World Geography: A Country by Country Guide*, Thunder Bay, San Diego, CA, 2003.

de Blij, H. J., and P. O. Muller, *Concepts and Regions in Geography*, John Wiley & Sons, New York, 2004.

Muller, P. O., and E. Muller-Hames, *Geography, Study Guide: Realms, Regions, and Concepts*, John Wiley & Sons, New York, 2005.

Oxford Atlas of the World, Oxford University Press, New York, 2003.

Parsons, J. (ed.), *Geography of the World*, DK Children, London and New York, 2006.

Peoples of the World: Their Cultures, Traditions, and Ways of Life, National Geographic, Washington, DC, 2001.

Pulsipher, L. M., *World Regional Geography: Global Patterns, Local Lives*, W. H. Freeman, New York, 2005.

Warf, B. (ed.), *Encyclopedia of Human Geography*, Sage Publications, London and New York, 2006.

Specific to this volume

Allan, T., *Ancient China*, Chelsea House Publications, New York, 2007.

Amery, H. A., and A. T. Wolf, *Water in the Middle East: A Geography of Peace*, University of Texas Press, Austin, TX, 2000.

Blunden, C., and M. Elvin, *Cultural Atlas of China*, Checkmark Books, New York, 1998.

Collcutt, M., and M. Jensen, *Cultural Atlas of Japan*, Checkmark Books, New York, 1988.

Cumings, B., *Korea's Place in the Sun: A Modern History*, W. W. Norton, New York, 2005.

Gilsenan, M., *Recognizing Islam: Religion and Society in the Modern Middle East* (rev. edn.), Tauris, New York, 2000.

Goldschmidt, Jr., A., Telhami, S., and K. Yambert (ed.), *The Contemporary Middle East*, Westview Press, Boulder, CO, 2006.

Gupta, A., *The Physical Geography of Southeast Asia*, Oxford University Press, New York, 2005.

Held, C. C., *Middle East Patterns: Places, Peoples, and Politics*, Westview Press, Boulder, CO, 2005.

Madsen, S. T. (ed.), *State, Society and the Environment in South Asia* (volume 3), Curzon Press, Richmond, UK, 1999.

Shahgedanova, M. (ed.), *The Physical Geography of Northern Eurasia*, Oxford University Press, New York, 2003.

Smith, C. J., *China: People and Places in the Land of One Billion*, Westview Press, Boulder, CO, 2007.

Varley, P., *Japanese Culture* (4th edn.), University of Hawaii Press, Honolulu, 2000.

Weightman, B., *Dragons and Tigers: A Geography of South, East and Southeast Asia*, John Wiley & Sons, Toronto, 2005.

Zhao, S., *Geography of China: Environment, Resources, Population, and Development*, John Wiley & Sons, Hoboken, NJ, 1994.

General Web Sites

www.ethnologue.com
A comprehensive guide to all the languages of the world.

www.factmonster.com/ipka/A0770414.html
Geography facts and figures for kids.

www.geographic.org
Information on geography for students, teachers, parents, and children.

www.odci.gov/cia/publications/factbook/index.html
Central Intelligence Agency factbook of country profiles.

ww.panda.org
World Wide Fund for Nature (WWF).

www.peoplegroups.org/default.aspx
Listing and information on major ethnic groups around the world.

www.worldatlas.com
A world atlas of facts, flags, and maps.

Web sites specific to this volume

www.aseansec.org
Web site of the Association of Southeast Asian Nations (ASEAN).

www.asiasociety.org
Home page of the Asia Society, an international educational organization dedicated to strengthening relationships and deepening understanding among the peoples of Asia and the United States

INDEX